To Tell a Story

John Berger was born in London in 1926. His seminal *Ways of Seeing* was one of the most influential books on art in the twentieth century. His many books, innovative in form and far-reaching in their historical and political insight, include *To the Wedding*, *King* and the Booker Prize-winning novel, *G*. He died, aged ninety, in January 2017.

Susan Sontag was born in Manhattan in 1933. Her non-fiction works include *Against Interpretation*, *On Photography*, *Illness as Metaphor*, *AIDS and its Metaphors*, *Regarding the Pain of Others* and *At the Same Time*. She was also the author of four novels, including *The Volcano Lover* and *In America*, as well as a collection of stories and several plays. In 2001 she was awarded the Jerusalem Prize for the body of her work and in 2003 she received the Prince of Asturias Award for Literature and the Peace Prize of the German Book Trade. She died in December 2004.

Benoît Bourreau is a writer and filmmaker based in Paris. His cinematic work primarily focuses on the aesthetics of art and its legacy, exploring the narratives rooted in memory.

To Tell a Story

John Berger

Susan Sontag

Edited by Benoît Bourreau

CANONGATE

First published in Great Britain as a Canon in 2026
by Canongate Books Ltd, 14 High Street, Edinburgh EH1 1TE

canongate.co.uk

1

Copyright © John Berger Estate and Susan Sontag Estate, 2026
Edition, Prologue and Epilogue © Benoît Bourreau, 2026
Translation from the French © Lily Robert-Foley, 2026

The right of John Berger, Susan Sontag and Benoît Bourreau to be identified as the authors of this work has been asserted by them in accordance with the Copyright, Designs and Patents Act 1988

Canongate supports copyright, which exists to encourage creativity by making sure that authors, artists and other creative people can be fairly rewarded for their work. Copyright allows authors control over the use and reproduction of their work. No part of this book may be used or reproduced in any manner for the purpose of training artificial intelligence technologies or systems. Canongate expressly reserves this work from text and data mining (Article 4(3) Directive (EU) 2019/790). By buying books (as well as borrowing them from the library) you are supporting authors and publishers and making new and original work possible.

Berger cover image by Jean Mohr, courtesy of Agencia Balcells
Sontag cover image by Brownie Harris, courtesy of Getty
For interior image credits please see p. 149

British Library Cataloguing-in-Publication Data
A catalogue record for this book is available on
request from the British Library

ISBN 978 1 83726 296 0

Typeset in F Grotesk Book by Palimpsest Book Production Ltd,
Falkirk, Stirlingshire

Printed and bound by CPI Group (UK) Ltd, Croydon CR0 4YY

The manufacturer's authorised representative in the EU for product safety is BGC Sustainability & Compliance, 7 avenue du Général Leclerc, Paris 75014 (gpsr@baldwinglobalconsulting.com)

Contents

Prologue 1

To Tell a Story 7

Send me Something 55

Between Self & System 111

Epilogue 141

Acknowledgements 147

Image Credits 149

Prologue
Benoît Bourreau

John Berger and Susan Sontag are both undoubtedly iconic figures of the intellectual effervescence of the second half of the twentieth century. They played an important role in the redefining of our relationship to all manner of cultural fields and remain major references in the turbulence of today's world. And though a significant connection existed between them, it remains largely unknown beyond their legendary televised conversation *To Tell a Story*.

Aired in 1983 as part of British television's Channel 4 programs, the event brought together Susan Sontag and John Berger for a dialogue on the art of narration, from its oral tradition to its deconstruction in modernity. This interview marks a formal milestone in media history, providing a counter-narrative to emergent storytelling trends and pre-empting the crucial aesthetic questions of the coming era. Rarely indeed are moments of such intellectual depth addressed directly to the public during prime-time television.

Currently housed in the British Film Institute collections, the video material of their discussion is available online. The surprising oratorical joust is divided into three acts and offers a very deliberately constructed argument. The affinities between Susan Sontag and John Berger are undeniable, fluctuating with their agreements and disagreements. Beyond the positions each of them upholds during the debate, their subtextual intimations are likewise telling.

As a great admirer of this broadcast, I wished to understand how it came about by retracing the relationship between the two authors. Echoing and opposing one another for the sake of argument, Susan Sontag and John Berger wonderfully exploit the freedom television had at that time. Paradoxically, it is through this medium that two personalities of the written word partially redefined their roles as narrators.

This decision is particularly fascinating. Why do John Berger and Susan Sontag choose in this instance to speak about stories, rather than about art or photography for example, for which both were already recognised as major thinkers? And more importantly, their opposition, often played up for the camera, betrays a complicity some time in the making . . . When and how had they met? What was their relationship like? And how long had it been going on?

Published in this volume for the first time, the transcript of *To Tell a Story* was a project originally commissioned by the *Times Literary Supplement*, but the project was eventually abandoned by its producer Udi Eichler. The program aired a decade after Berger and Sontag's first encounter and their talk at one of the renowned International Design Conferences in Aspen (IDCA), to which an audio recording conserved at the Getty Research Institute bears witness. These documents, brought together and accompanied by letters uncovered in the personal archives of the two authors at UCLA and in Quincy, bring context to their historical bond.

Susan Sontag and John Berger surely knew of each other by reputation from their first publications in the middle of the 1960s. A contribution by Susan Sontag appeared in the book *Authors Take Sides on Vietnam: Two Question on the War in Vietnam, Answered by the Authors of Several Nations* published in New York in 1967, and in January of that same year John Berger gave a speech at Oxford Vietnam Week which was later published as a pamphlet in London under the title *Let Vietnam Live!*

But it is in the heart of the Colorado Rockies that John Berger and Susan Sontag met for the first time at the occasion of their invitation to the twenty-fourth edition of the IDCA, which took place from 16–21 of June in 1974. Inspired by the spirit of Bauhaus, the mission of the conference from its start in 1951 was to bring artists and intellectuals together for a week around a different theme each year. That year's conference was entitled 'Between Self & System' and the programme announced activist Bobby Seale, writer Wole Soyinka, scientist Jerome Lettwin, painter Otto Piene, filmmaker Pier Paolo Pasolini, architect Kishō Kurikawa, designer Milton Glaser, and photographer Cornell Capa, among others.

According to the Aspen Records, John Berger was scheduled to present two extracts from *Ways of Seeing* on the evening of 17 June, followed the next afternoon by a discussion on his famous series on art produced in 1972 by the BBC. As for Susan Sontag, she was due to give a talk on the morning of the 18th followed the next evening by a screening of *Promised Lands,* a documentary filmed the year before at the end of the Yom Kippur war. On the first day, however, controversy decided otherwise.

At the conclusion of a lively presentation as part of *The Concerned Photographer 2* exhibition by Cornell Capa that afternoon, Susan Sontag and John Berger suggested an in-conversation event between the two of them the next day followed by a Q&A instead of their previously planned talks. It was in this rather impromptu fashion, and after barely having met, that the two of them found themselves together, facing a reasonably agitated assembly, to debate the impact of photography in contemporary society.

After this formative moment, their relationship took an episodic epistolary form. Their exchange grew more frequent in 1978, when Susan Sontag published her essay *On Photography*, which John Berger reviewed several times, refining and expanding his critiques leading up to the publication in 1980 of his own work, *About Looking*. These writings made their mark on Susan Sontag, who was turning her attention at that period more pointedly to the novel. The letters came less frequently after this but continued until 1998 and shed light in a more intimate manner on certain of their reciprocal influences.

The question of narration, already present in their exchanged reflections on photography, became central during the televised debate on 9 February 1983. Susan Sontag was in post-production on her film *Letter from Venice* when John Berger invited her to appear with him on *Voices*, a brand-new show devoted to the life of art and ideas, whose later episodes include as their guests the critic Al Alvarez, sociologist Richard Sennett, philosopher André Gorz, writer Umberto Eco . . . *To Tell a Story* is a unique episode in the series insofar as the two interlocutors are viewed in a discussion led by themselves alone.

The reverse-chronological reading offered through this book will, I hope, create access for the first time to the shared history of Susan Sontag and John Berger. In juxtaposition with the captivating and performative aura of *To Tell a Story*, the simple and direct correspondence which spreads out in skips and jumps over nearly a quarter of a century, as well as the impromptu nature of their first event together in Aspen, will paint a better picture of all the concerns at the heart of their work.

This volume contains composite and fragmentary material from an audiovisual program, rare and precious letters, and a sound recording. It thus remains elliptical and does not pretend to encompass the entirety of their longstanding connection that is also made up of shared readings and conversations, meetings across sojourns and travels, but also of present and missing moments, or simply phone calls. What this diversity of circumstances, sources and temporalities does show, however, is the intensity of an artistic friendship in perpetual motion. Lively and sometimes even trivial, the voices of John Berger and Susan Sontag lead us back through these pages in polyphonic echoes to their respective bodies of work.

To Tell a Story

Voices, 1983

Conversation between John Berger and Susan Sontag,
filmed on 1 February 1983 and broadcast on 9 February 1983
as part of the British television programme *Voices* on
Channel 4, 1-inch C-format master videotape from BFI.

Part One

JOHN BERGER
(to the audience)

> Good evening. Tonight, *Voices* is a little different, because there are only two of us, Susan Sontag and myself, John Berger. Susan and I have quite a lot of things in common, I think. We both write essays, about literature, about ideas. We both have worked for films. Susan has just come back from Rome, where she's been making a film based on one of her own short stories. I've written film scenarios. We've both from time to time written quite a lot about photography, about the visual photographic image. And then finally, and perhaps most important of all for tonight, we both write fiction, novels and short stories. And tonight, we're going to exchange views and experiences about this activity – somewhat mysterious, really – this activity of telling stories.

JOHN BERGER

(turning to SUSAN SONTAG)

> If I think of somebody telling a story, I see a group of people, huddled together, and around them a vast space, quite frightening. Maybe they are huddled against a wall, maybe they're round a fire, and somewhere for me, in the very idea of the story, there is something to do with shelter. The shelter, perhaps of the voyager, the traveller who has come home, who has lived to tell the story, or the soldier who has come back, who has survived. So, there is this almost physical sense of shelter, where the story represents a kind of habitation, a kind of home. But then, inside the story there's another kind of shelter. Because what the story narrates and tells is sheltered within the story, from oblivion, forgetfulness and daily indifference—

SUSAN SONTAG

(interrupting him)

> But you're talking about stories in a very, umm, remote kind of society that's quite different from ours, because surely storytelling is much more diversified in the societies that we know. Parents tell stories to children. Children ask for stories. We experience stories mediated through images, as in television and movies. We read stories in print. I think that the most archaic definition of storytelling – it does tell us something about what we imagine where storytelling comes from, but it doesn't tell us very much about what stories have become, I think, or what the challenge of storytelling is now.

JOHN BERGER

Yes, I agree, but I'm not certain that something of that primitive origin doesn't remain. For instance, when children hear stories, or when we were children and they told us stories, when does it happen? In bed, in this strange no man's land between waking and sleep, and in that telling of a story, or listening to a story, there is something reassuring. And very curious, because the more exciting, the more frightening the story, the more reassuring it is. Why?

SUSAN SONTAG

But John, don't you think that people make a distinction between a story that is true, and a story that is imagined or invented? I'm always struck by the fact that there's a kind of ambiguity in the very notion of storytelling. On the one hand, we think of storytelling as a truth-telling activity – tell me the real story. We think of stories as bringing information. We think of stories as revealing secrets. True stories that might be told after someone's death, because for instance the death of someone is generally an occasion for telling stories about a person's life and maybe some truth comes out that wasn't discussed or generally shared before that person was gone. But we also think of stories as: 'that's only a story', 'oh don't tell me stories' – meaning don't tell me lies. And don't you think at the very centre of the whole enterprise of storytelling there is the fact that storytelling is an activity that faces in two directions? On the one hand, it's connected with an idea of truth. On the other hand, it's connected with an idea of invention, imagination, lies. One is thrilled by the story precisely because it describes something that can't happen, it's connected with fantasy, I think it's also so complicated and the model of the voyager, or the returning soldier, who was telling what really happened to his bringing exotic news and telling terrible stories generally is only one model of storytelling.

JOHN BERGER

Yes, yes. I don't want to insist too much upon that, and probably those stories were very embroidered. Yes, umm, the story exists somewhere between fiction and truth, I agree. If I think now straight away of my own personal experience in telling stories or writing stories, I think they begin off for me, and they have to begin off, as truth. For instance, I won't tell you the whole story but a little one . . . A man I knew in the village where I live, a shepherd, with about a hundred sheep, and he fell in love. He fell in love with a woman, married, not from the village, from the town. A long love affair, for a couple of years, very passionate, probably with the complicity of the husband. And the woman, well, he gave her many things – half of what he had at least, including a house. And then she, she turned him out, and he decided to die. He didn't kill himself, he went on a kind of hunger strike, and then he died. When I think of him now I can see his face, his very large hands, his eyes. That was truth. Then I tried to write that story—

SUSAN SONTAG
(interrupting him)
And then you started inventing.

JOHN BERGER

> I started inventing, but in relation to the truth. But, but if it worked, if it worked – I don't know – this story will be read as fiction, and it will be read as fiction about a story of more or less unrequited love. And why would it be fiction? Because it will exist both everywhere and nowhere. And it is that displacement of place and time which makes something fiction, it seems to me.

SUSAN SONTAG

> But why would it be read as taking place everywhere and nowhere? Don't you situate it in the village where you live?

JOHN BERGER

> For me it's situated in the village. But as soon as one reads a story, no, when we read other people's stories, we have an idea of that place but, it becomes part of our experience and therefore is displaced from where it really took place, and it seems to me the fiction is something which exists, umm, which goes beyond its immediate time or its immediate place, and it's exactly that which makes it fiction, or what we call fiction.

SUSAN SONTAG

> I don't have that experience, I think. Well of course it's true that I'm not where the story is taking place, but if you're talking about some kind of traditional storytelling, which is grounded in a particular place, if I read a story of Tolstoy . . .

JOHN BERGER
(nodding)
> Yes . . .

SUSAN SONTAG
> . . . I think I'm in nineteenth-century or early twentieth-century Russia. I don't think it's taking place everywhere—

JOHN BERGER
(interrupting her)
> But it applies to you and your experience of life.

SUSAN SONTAG
> Not necessarily. No, it might instruct my experience rather than apply to it. I mean I'm not looking to see myself projected in stories, any more than I'm trying to express myself when I write stories. No, I don't think stories are necessarily universal because they're read by very different kinds of people. Some stories – because one of the most powerful forms of storytelling is very compact, and if it's very compact it's likely to be very economical in its details, and therefore this economy can be experienced by us with our modern ways of looking at things as something abstract, and in that sense, it may take on a certain universality. But I think it is the particularity of storytelling, and the fact that we now have available to us stories from every part of the world, that fascinates us. And I don't ask that the story address my experience. I ask that my experience, so to speak, make it possible for me to understand the story.

JOHN BERGER
(reflexive, to himself)
>Yes . . .

SUSAN SONTAG
>I'm not looking for myself in this story. I think I have maybe another way of looking at it from you because I really start not from the oral tradition, but from the literary tradition. If I think of storytelling, let's say that the parent of the child now usually in our society is reading a story rather than telling a story, we have so many stories available to us in fact. Sometimes people say that we have a surfeit of stories, which is why storytelling is often thought to be in a state of crisis. And so my model is originally a literary model. And I'm a city dweller. And you're someone who has lived a large part of your life, though you grew up as I understand in London, in a peasant community in the South of France. And therefore you feel closer by choice, because you've chosen to live there, to another what many people would think of as an older form of storytelling, which is oral, and you have the stories of these people's lives whom you come to know, and you want to tell their stories to other people because there's I think an ethical assumption behind your work, that there are stories which have not been told, certain kinds of people in certain kinds of experience which have not found voice, and you want to give voice to experiences which are neglected, or regenerate, or revive certain forms of storytelling which are neglected now in favour of perhaps more sophisticated, city-oriented, print-oriented kinds of storytelling. Isn't that what you're

saying when you told this fascinating story about the shepherd and his unrequited love, and his kind of suicide? The reason you wanted to tell the story is that you were moved by him. And he was a kind of person that perhaps you don't find in our literature as much any more, although obviously there are, I mean one only has to go back to [Thomas] Hardy if not to other examples to find stories of that kind, but perhaps they're not told today as often. And so, don't you feel that some stories should be told rather than other stories? Isn't that behind your attitude towards storytelling?

JOHN BERGER

I think it's less, perhaps . . . it's less sociological than that. It doesn't really concern me whether that kind of story exists in literature or not. If I'm very, very honest. I mean it is because that life was lived. I see a kind of meaning in it, and I would like to retain it. So that it is not lost, not forgotten. I mean, whether we're telling stories in a city context or in a village, probably you'll agree that in fact stories begin at their end. I mean in life. I mean the story of Romeo and Juliet in a sense begins at their death, that is when the story is given form. The end is not always death, but it quite frequently is, umm—

SUSAN SONTAG

(interrupting him)

That's a point I think that's worth talking about! Why death seems the natural end of a story – and in the most traditional form of storytelling I think that it is. Is it because death is the natural end of a life? And what stories are about our lives? See, I think they're about much more than that, but that is certainly one model of storytelling: to tell the story of a life, to give the value of a life in the form of a story which has its natural end as a death. But if I think for instance of the first stories that I remember reading, which really marked me as a person and undoubtedly as a writer too, were the stories of Edgar Allan Poe. And those are not stories of a life but they are real stories, absolutely unforgettable stories. They are stories generally of a disaster, which may or may not end in death – it often does, but they are terrifying stories, they are fabulous stories, and on the whole they are invented stories. The storyteller is the person who invents. We have examples of that now in writers like Calvino and Borges who certainly think of themselves as storytellers, but they're not telling stories of lives, they're telling stories of dilemmas, let's say, which often are catastrophes. What about that kind of storytelling as opposed to rendering a life? It's quite another model and it's one that interests me very much.

JOHN BERGER

I think that the fantastic story – what does it tell us? I mean, you tell me. What is our need for the fantastic story? We have it, I agree with you. I agree with you. But why?

SUSAN SONTAG

Well, I think people want to travel outside themselves. I think there's a need for vicarious experience that is not necessarily identical with the need for truth. I think there's a need for fantasy. I think there is a longing to see taboos broken, violated. There is . . . The imagination runs riot, and I think *that* kind of storytelling is very important. I must say it does appeal more to me. I always feel when I'm writing stories that I'm inventing and I might use something from my own life, or the life of someone I know. But I feel as if I'm lending that to something that is basically invented, and therefore basically fantastic. And I think of fiction – but, again, I'm just speaking for myself and thinking of examples of fiction that I like very much – I think of fiction as a kind of speculativeness, a kind of fantasy. I'm interested in moral fantasies, moral science fiction even, and this could have the form of some kind of history or actually be placed in the past, as well as in the future or in the present.

JOHN BERGER

If we take the experience of writing a story, or of listening to one, it seems to me every story has its own subjectivity. And I emphasise that because I think this subjectivity is an area where what you call the truthful and the fantastic actually coexist, because it is a subjectivity.

SUSAN SONTAG

Do you mean a voice?

JOHN BERGER

Well, a voice, in a minute, Susan, we must talk about that, but no I mean a kind of subjectivity. Now it seems to me the subjectivity is a kind of amalgam of three elements, or three people: the storyteller or the writer, the protagonists of the story and their subjectivity, and then lastly the subjectivity of the listener. And the story – there is already a kind of cooperation between these three, which actually makes the subjectivity of that story.

SUSAN SONTAG

That's very strange to me what you're saying, because I can't feel the subjectivity of the listener or the reader. To me that is a – of course I think if I write a story it will be read, I wouldn't write if I didn't think that I could be read – but I can't imagine how that could actually be part of the story.

JOHN BERGER

When you were a child, remember listening to stories? And who were you? You were yourself? You were the person telling you the story? And you were the characters, all mixed together in a rather assuring way!

SUSAN SONTAG

Maybe that's because I think the difference between hearing stories and reading them is greater than you do . . .

(to the audience)

We have to stop now and we'll be back in a moment.

Part Two

JOHN BERGER
> Susan, you were making a distinction between the printed story, literature, and the spoken story, the oral tradition. And you're saying that I'm more embedded in the second than in the first. Now I think that is only apparently so, because—

SUSAN SONTAG
(interrupting him)
> Only apparently so that you're embedded in the second?

JOHN BERGER
> Yes, only apparently so, because they're not oral. I want them to be read as though they were spoken but they are not, and they've never been spoken. And all the devices I use are in fact literary devices. I mean, that's to say they're devices that I have learnt

from my experience of literature and of reading masters, so it is a form, but it is in fact a literary form.

SUSAN SONTAG

No, but I'm not denying that you're making literature when you tell, say, the story about the peasant, the shepherd who commits suicide when he's thrown out by the woman he loves. I'm saying that you are trying to equate telling a story with writing a story. In other words, you're saying writing is a kind of telling. Writing is the telling with art, so to speak. It's a transformation of oral telling. What I'm saying, and that I think is one of the points on which we disagree, is I think that once people began to write stories, they told different kinds of stories, that there was a radical break with the oral tradition, that there are things that you can tell in a written form. They're things you want to tell in a written form, which you couldn't tell in an oral form. For instance, I know in my own story-writing, I'm very interested in telling several stories at the same time, and sometimes cutting back from one to another. I suppose it's something that I learned not only from literature, but more obviously from movies.

JOHN BERGER

Yes!

SUSAN SONTAG

From cutting in movies, cutting back from one shot to another or keeping several stories going at the same time – the famous model is Griffiths' *Intolerance*. But that's the kind of thing that you can't do orally, so I really think there is a radical break. It's not just the addition of art or artfulness but a tremendous expansion and modification of storytelling that comes when you have the resources of print and when you are reading with the eyes, as opposed to hearing with the ears.

JOHN BERGER

Yes, all right, you're trying to tell several stories at the same time and it's a bit like editing a film, it's a bit like montage.

SUSAN SONTAG

Mm-hm . . .

JOHN BERGER

But that exists, I think, in any form of story because, and let's be technical almost, because of what is not said.

SUSAN SONTAG

Mm-hm . . .

JOHN BERGER

So important! What happens between the sentences, even sometimes between the words. You have a sentence, 'he went out of the house and left the door open'. That's one sentence. As soon as a second sentence is put on to that, which is, umm, 'the mad dog was in the orchard . . .'

SUSAN SONTAG

You have a cut!

JOHN BERGER

You have a cut . . .

SUSAN SONTAG
> Yeah!

JOHN BERGER
> ... Because the door is open and the mad dog is in the orchard!

SUSAN SONTAG
> Mm-hm ...

JOHN BERGER
> This happens whether a story is told orally, whether it is written – if it is well told. There are always these jumps. And through the duration of the story, a kind of complicity is built up. Because each one of those jumps is based upon certain assumptions, which the writer makes about the reader's reactions, and bit by bit these assumptions are more and more taken for granted, and you begin to have this complicity between storyteller or writer, and reader or listener.

SUSAN SONTAG
> But isn't it just that you can't say everything. I mean if you would tell the story of a day, not even a day, an hour in anyone's life, you could write a thousand pages. So, in storytelling as in every other form of art, there's a process of selection. But if the person goes out to the door and leaves the house, and leaves the door – exits from the house and leaves the door open – and then you cut to the mad dog in the orchard, it's only two stories. If you're going to follow the man somewhere else and then also tell a long story about the dog, the assumption is that the man and the dog will meet, that the dog in the

orchard has something to do with the man. But you don't describe step by step as he goes down the walk and goes toward the orchard or avoids the orchard, or whatever it is. I mean I don't think that constitutes telling many stories, the fact that from one sentence to the next you are featuring a different detail, and in fact you're skipping time. You're skipping all sorts of things that you could be telling. The question is of course what kind of detail are we interested in telling. And there we have a very particular set of traditions that we're responsive to as writers. For instance, since Flaubert we have been very interested, as writers and as readers, and very moved by a sort of off-centre detail, an unexpected detail. Flaubert in *Madame Bovary* describing Charles looking at the back of Emma's neck for instance, or the angle of her elbow as she poured a pitcher of milk. We look for the angular or the eccentric detail, as illustrating what? As illustrating the story or as having in fact I think some kind of autonomy, some sort of independent sensual effect which is what we're looking for in storytelling. That's a particular literary tradition. I mean if you read Defoe, if you read *Moll Flanders* for instance, you're not going to get that kind of detail that you get many literary generations later in someone like Flaubert.

JOHN BERGER

In the choosing, in the selecting, one chooses what one judges to be essential. Because when I go back to my beginning, it seems to me that all fiction is a fight against the absurd.

SUSAN SONTAG
(kindly mocking)
> Is that your beginning?!

JOHN BERGER
(laughs)
> Well, it was behind my beginning, it was the end of my beginning! Because in a dream, for example, dreams can be terrifying, nightmares, but in a dream there is nothing which does not have a signification. And I'm not talking now about psychoanalytical explanations afterwards. I mean in the dreaming state, everything that one sees, everything that happens has a meaning. There is nothing which is meaningless. Because that is the way our minds are structured, and it seems to me it is the same in fiction. If it works, if it is really viable, everything that is included has a meaning. Not necessarily an explicit one, but an implicit one.

SUSAN SONTAG
> Yes, I don't agree with that. I mean I think that what happens in dreaming, as in anything else, is that once you have the narration, or once you have the event, then you can always assign meaning to it. And you want to assign meaning to it. But I don't think the meaning resides in the details. I don't think that every event in a dream has meaning. I think you can impute meaning to it, you can assign meaning to it.

JOHN BERGER
> No, you experience it as meaning in the dream. I'm not talking about the interpretation of the dream afterwards.

SUSAN SONTAG

I don't think you experience anything. Well, here we have a real disagreement, because I think that the dream – and I'm surprised I'm taking this position, I would think you would take it! – I think in fact that the dream is the telling of the dream. I don't think the dream exists, or as soon as it exists it doesn't exist. But what does exist is the already highly selective account that you make of the dream to yourself, writing it out or to someone else saying I had this incredible dream last night, and then as you begin to talk about it, you say well actually that old woman reminded me of my aunt, and actually the chair in that room was a chair in the dormitory in the school that I went to when I was nine years old, and you begin to find associations. And I think that makes the kind of meaning that we – that's a very simple level of meaning that we assign to dreams. And even in stories, I don't know that I would say that every detail has to be essential. I would say that every detail has to be powerful, every detail has to be thrilling and then after the fact, because a story should have some quality of inevitability or necessity. And perhaps it's that that we then say gives it some essential quality.

JOHN BERGER

No, I mean, I think we differ because for me a story is always a rescuing operation. Which is another way of saying a shelter.

SUSAN SONTAG
(doubtful)

Well, of the absurd?

JOHN BERGER

Against the absurd. Against that endless terrifying space in which we live. I mean, let's go back.

SUSAN SONTAG

I don't understand that. Why does it rescue us from the absurd? Why?

JOHN BERGER

Because it is preserved! Because that experience which the story relates, and it doesn't matter whether it is invented or based on fact. I mean that is always a false question. And it is always an extraordinary mixture one with the other, you know, I mean what do you invent, what is real, it's not interesting, I'm sure. But it is something in actual fact which somewhere, somehow, has been lived. In being related – and the word is interesting, 'related', or if you like 'narrating', but let's say 'related' – in being related, it is given meaning. It is given meaning, partly because everything in it is related, one thing to another. It becomes coherent. It is given form. And the meaning, of course, because otherwise the story merely becomes extremely didactic – it isn't that it imposes a meaning upon the story. But the story contains a meaning. When I wrote the story you know called 'The Three Lives of Lucie Cabrol', which is a story about a peasant woman and the first life is about her childhood, and the second life is about her middle age, and the third life is about what happens to her after death. In the village where I live, quite a lot of friends, peasants, read this and not only once but twice or three times they made the same remark to me. They said, well, you know in fact Lucy Cabrol has four lives. I say, what? Yes, because she has her fourth life in your story. And it wasn't a literary compliment, that's the important thing!

SUSAN SONTAG

Now I know why you think of audience in a way that I don't. If you were actually reading your stories to people who know the characters on whom they're based, of course you have an experience which is extremely rare for a contemporary writer. When I write a story, I'm sure that I don't have a privileged first audience, in the sense that I'm not part of a small community in the way that you are. And I'm not telling a story that people will immediately recognise as part of their experience. I mean in a way you're more like, oh let's say, a Soviet writer, telling stories about the gulag and know that part of his audience will be people who have been in those camps, and will be judging his story by the criteria of their own experience. It was really like that. And at last this person is really telling the world how it was for us. I think that's, I mean, it's very admirable and very moving, but it is still only one kind of story-telling. There is another kind of storytelling which I think is freer of that kind of ethical responsibility which you're assuming is part of the storyteller's vocation, and which gives that essential quality to storytelling. I think, for instance, one could reverse what you're saying, and say not that the story redeems reality, as if reality has no meaning, but the storyteller gives it meaning. But you could say simply that – or not simply – that the storyteller enlarges the field of our imagination and introduces us to the absurd. Because on the contrary, it's not that we live in terror of the absurd but rather we live . . .

JOHN BERGER

(quite suspicious)

Don't they?!

SUSAN SONTAG

No. I don't think most people do! I think rather we live with our imagination very quiet, very still, at least after a certain age. And with all kinds of terrible conformities which make much more—

JOHN BERGER

(interrupting her)

Why terrible? But why terrible? because they suggest the absurd!

SUSAN SONTAG

No! because they deprive us or cut us off from the life of the mind and the life of the imagination. And that perhaps one of the functions of storytelling, I would say, is to introduce a sense of the fantastic, which might include the absurd, rather than to redeem reality from its absurd or meaningless aspect. I don't think that stories necessarily have meaning. In fact I don't even know what that means. I don't know. I'll tell you the last three works of fiction which I read – that's completely arbitrary. None of these books are modern. The last three books of fiction I read were *Villette* by Charlotte Brontë, *Berger's Daughter – Burger's Daughter*, rather. I'm mixing it up with your name, John!

– *Burger's Daughter* by Nadine Gordimer, and *Flush* by Virginia Woolf. Now all three of these books of fiction tell stories. Flush tells the story of the Brownings viewed from through the eyes of the cocker spaniel that belonged to Elizabeth Barrett – she eloped with it when she went with Robert Browning. And *Villette*, which is the unknown wonderful novel by the author of *Jane Eyre*, tells a story of a schoolteacher in Brussels, based obviously on Charlotte Brontë's own experience when she was a very young woman. And the Nadine Gordimer novel tells the story of a woman, a young woman, in South Africa. I must say, all of these are stories, and yet it was character and hallucinatory detail in these stories. I mean the cocker spaniel in Florence smelling urine on the sidewalk and noticing the difference between Italian vegetables and London vegetables. Or in the Charlotte Brontë novel, it's extremely hallucinatory. One can almost say surrealistic in the account of this boarding school in Brussels. And the same for the best passages in Nadine Gordimer's book – and she's a wonderfully sensual writer. I don't think it was the story that interested me. It was being carried away by a character and being, feeling my imagination and my—

JOHN BERGER
(interrupting her)
    No, I mean, I think—

SUSAN SONTAG

(continuing)

> ... my sense of language raised to a new pitch by the art of language, and the way in which almost anything could be related by these three very different writers. That in fact all three of them told the story of a life was almost secondary, and I don't know what the meaning is, except to establish the rights of intensity. I think of that as the quality of fiction and storytelling. Restoring the claims of intensity, of intensity of feeling. I love a story that makes me cry, for instance. And I don't mean that it has to do with some meaning that I could sum up.

JOHN BERGER

> It seems to me, I mean yes, I think there, here we really differ. There is no intensity in a story which actually matches the intensity of what is lived. And I think we have two different views because you, in a way, you say you want to be carried away by the story. I'm saying I want the story to stop things being carried away into oblivion and into indifference. And you're right. I mean, the fact that I live in a village is very important for lots of reasons. We were talking earlier about death. Death as often being the end of the story, which is actually where the story begins. That's to say it's where one begins writing it, or telling it. Somebody dies. Now it's not just a question of *tact* that one then says, well perhaps it is possible to tell that story. It's not only that. That's a relatively superficial thing. It's because after that death—

SUSAN SONTAG

(thoughtful)

> The life is finished—

JOHN BERGER

(continuing)

> ... one can read that life. The life becomes readable.

SUSAN SONTAG

> Well a person who dies at thirty-seven is not the same as a person who dies at seventy-seven!

JOHN BERGER

> No, but it can be somebody who dies at ninety. The life becomes readable to the storyteller, or to the writer. And then she, or he, can begin to write that.

SUSAN SONTAG

> Well, that would make marriage, which is also another traditional, not contemporary ending for stories, equivalent to death. That is if one sees life as only having a meaning in your sense, because it leads up to something then, that it leads up to its end or it leads up to at least its transformation. Let's say, in the traditional way that marriage was viewed as a transformation.

JOHN BERGER

> Yes ... I mean, for example, I don't think it exists here in England but yes, I mean, you know the origin of the stag party before the marriage? I mean, that is in actual fact that the end of a certain part of life—

SUSAN SONTAG

Well, I was thinking of Shakespeare actually. If you could say that generally the comedies end in marriages and the tragedies end in deaths, both of them are endings in the sense that the life is seen as leading up to this, and whatever comes after is another life, another kind of life.

JOHN BERGER

But let me go back. It seems to me that a life becomes readable, and therefore recountable, when it has come to an end, which puts the writer or the storyteller into a strange category. I mean he's a kind of secretary of death. He's death secretary, very familiar. But what he reads of course is not death, but is life. He reads as it were across that blackness, and he begins to write. And there is a counter movement in time because life goes on in one direction, the story turns in the other. I mean, in those early Latin inscriptions, the very early ones, there's a term for it, what's it called *boustrophedon* or something like that . . . Anyway, it's 'as the ox turns in ploughing' because you had one line which went like that and then they didn't begin the other line there, but it went like that. So you have that movement. (draws a zig-zag).

SUSAN SONTAG

But do you really think that a life is only intelligible when it's over?! I don't think so . . .

JOHN BERGER

Intelligible, no.

SUSAN SONTAG

You can only read it?!

JOHN BERGER

No, its full meaning is only apparent. It's intelligible, it's understandable before, of course.

SUSAN SONTAG

But then you are saying that the central thing about storytelling is to tell a life, and if the maximal understanding of a life only comes after death, then the basic model of storytelling for you, of narration for you, is telling the story of a life. And that's, you see, where I don't agree. I mean, I think that's a very interesting model and I suppose it is an archaic model, not the only one. Because there are other stories that are told which don't involve simply a single life but involve, let's say, an event like a campaign in a war or something of that sort which often is punctuated by death. And I love your formulation that the writer is death's secretary. I think that's true. But I think it's true in a less literal way than you are suggesting. Because I guess I'd still baulk at the idea that the fundamental thing about storytelling is telling the story of a life or, I presume you would expand that to mean a series of lives of a family, could be a family or a community, or whatever. Don't you think there are many other kinds of storytelling? And don't you think that—

JOHN BERGER
(interrupting her)

Oh, I do!

SUSAN SONTAG
(continuing)
> ... there are lots of wonderful narrations whose central strength is the depiction of character, in which incident is relatively unimportant or only illustrative? I mean there's an awful lot of modern storytelling in which action is relatively immobilised. And what story there is, is almost presumed to be known and therefore the main part of the storytelling is really a comment on a story. A comment on something that one already knows to be happening. It's not in the 'and then, and then, and then' form. And I think this is a great achievement. I think we've enormously expanded the resources of storytelling. I don't feel as many people do that fiction is dead or that we have exhausted the possibilities of storytelling, or as we get further from older models, oral models, we are impoverishing ourselves. I think we're expanding the possibilities.

JOHN BERGER
> Yes ... Let me go back to something you said today. And I'm not arguing. I mean, I'm arguing from the point of view of, umm, my own point of view, as how I—

SUSAN SONTAG
> I'm arguing from my own point of view, too!

JOHN BERGER
> I know! But what I'm saying is not exhaustive. I mean, I think there are many other forms of storytelling. I have the feeling that mine is somewhere at the heart of the matter, but there are other forms.

The comment, I think that as soon as a story is printed, it – this is very important – as soon as a story is printed it is transportable. In a way that an oral story isn't. Therefore, it may be about one place, it may be written in one place but it can go to many places. And however faithful that story is to an imagined or a real life or series of lives or incidents, there is a kind of comment which needs to come in, and which is why the storyteller is necessary. Because if that story was told in reality by any of the protagonists, they would be seeing it completely from a center. The storyteller is both at the center, intimate, and at a distance, on the horizon. He is in a sort of way the horizon, with one side of him to the story, and the other side, which is going way, way beyond that place, that land, that time to the general. Maybe the only little contribution that the storyteller makes is to place stories in that context where – and that is terribly true now, in this twentieth century – where everybody lives in the whole world, across the whole planet—

SUSAN SONTAG
(interrupting him)

Hearing stories from everywhere—

JOHN BERGER
(continuing)

Yes, so that what happens is that that story, which may be some tiny little affair in some tiny village or some back street of a city, is somehow placed in the modern world. How – not by crude statements of comparison or historical argument, or political argument, it's a very, very, very subtle process – how, somehow, you have to give the feeling that what is being narrated there coexists in the world where China exists, and the Pacific Ocean, and there are men who have been to the moon.

SUSAN SONTAG

But I see a bigger and bigger difference between us, because you see the world as full of stories. And then you see these special people who constitute themselves as storytellers, and who now generally don't use the word, they say they're writers. And they tell these stories, they are the bearer of stories, they're the transmitters or emitters of stories.

JOHN BERGER

Vehicles!

SUSAN SONTAG

The vehicles. The secretaries if you will. The secretary of stories. The secretaries of death. I don't see that the world is full of stories in that sense. I mean, I think the story starts with the writer. I don't think that there is a story and then the writer claims it, and transforms it, and puts his or her voice into it and adds this subjectivity. I think the writer is to begin with the originator of stories. And there are no stories outside of literature.

JOHN BERGER

(to the audience)

Let me stop there for a moment, and we'll go on.

Part Three

JOHN BERGER

Susan, we both write essays and we both write fiction. For me, in fact, the two activities are not very different.

SUSAN SONTAG

How?

JOHN BERGER

Well, first of all, I'm not very verbal. Really, I have no facility with words.

SUSAN SONTAG

I don't believe that for a minute . . .

JOHN BERGER

No, it's true. It's true, and the struggle for me to write anything, essay or fiction, is always that there is a kind of model of something that I've seen, or something that I've perceived in some way or another. It may be in a life, it may be in a film, or it may be in a painting, or a work of literature, somebody else's . . . Something which I feel which is almost by definition unsayable, which exists there, or a bit like a melody of music, a bit like a pattern of colours, sometimes a bit like a geometric form. And the struggle is always to try to recreate that in words. The struggle is a question of precision. So that finally the words are as close as possible – they're never close enough, but as close as possible – to that model which is nonverbal, which I have felt, intuited, perceived, sensed. And it's not very different when I'm writing about a work of art, or whether I'm writing about a banquet, or a wedding party, or a death.

SUSAN SONTAG

Mmm, well it's not the same for me. When I write essays and when I write stories, it seems to me an entirely different activity. In fact I really have the impression that I have to sort of take my head off and put another head on, in order to do this. I mean, what they have in common is the struggle. Of course, writing is a very painful activity and it's very difficult.

JOHN BERGER

There are more painful ones!

SUSAN SONTAG

I'm sure, but there are less painful ones too! I mean, I wouldn't say that the struggle – that we all feel inarticulate – but we also are, John, let's face it, we are also very verbal people. And we talk all the time.

We don't talk as well as we write, of course, but that's by definition, I think, what writing is about – to be better than talk.

JOHN BERGER

(teasing)

It's a replay.

SUSAN SONTAG

Well, you get to rewrite. You don't get to retalk. But you do get to rewrite, but I do think of them as very different activities because I guess I don't have this model of truth-telling, or of chronicling, which seems to underlie everything that you said about writing fiction or about storytelling.

JOHN BERGER

How does the story begin for you?

SUSAN SONTAG

Well, let me just go back one step further. I mean, I think that when I write an essay, I am certainly . . . The motive for an essay is certainly something that I perceive, or think about, or it's a set of problems which generates another set of problems and another and another and another and then, I find a pretext to talk about these problems in a particular work of art, or situation, or idea, or whatever. But when I'm writing an essay, I am asking myself all the time, is it true what I'm saying? I mean, it is really like that? And that is the same question as, can I say it better? But the question of how I can say it better, in a more complex, or subtle, or eloquent way – that question is identical with, or goes side by side with the question of whether what I'm saying is actually true!

invention, and one intimately connected with language, with tone, with voice.

JOHN BERGER

And maybe – it's very interesting that, because it is once more and we've often touched upon this. Because maybe we arrive at something quite similar, but it is the reverse process. I mean, for me, there's never that voice at the beginning. There is the enormous difficulty of seeing that situation, that person—

SUSAN SONTAG

Oh, I don't see, I hear!

JOHN BERGER

No, I see, and . . .

SUSAN SONTAG

That's perhaps why I'd like to make movies, because I don't see. I only hear when I write, and therefore I want very much to see. And that, I like to do with images more than with language.

JOHN BERGER

And when that person is really there, which is probably in the real time of writing somewhere around about two thirds. Not necessarily two thirds of the text, but two thirds of the writing time, in the months or the years. Then, suddenly, the voices come. And then I just write. But they come after the situation or the people have been established, not before.

SUSAN SONTAG

No, for me the people come out of the language. I feel them.

JOHN BERGER

>For me, the language comes out of the people.

SUSAN SONTAG

>I think my attitude is really . . . Well, for one thing, I mean, it's very clear from our conversation that I'm really loyal to certain modernist assumptions about art, about literature, which I think you have come to question and abandon the practice of. Because I think of an earlier work of fiction of yours, like your novel *G.* You were doing then something that is closer to what I continue to do as a fiction writer. But the stories that you've been writing recently about peasant life are, I think – I don't know whether you feel that – in a very different mode, or a very different model . . .

JOHN BERGER

>Because the subject is so different, I think. It's true.

SUSAN SONTAG

>But haven't you changed, John? Haven't you yourself changed?

JOHN BERGER

>I don't know. I've had to relearn to write, that's true. Because the experience of the underprivileged, or of peasants, is very different from the experience of the privileged – and *G.* is a book about them.

SUSAN SONTAG

>But do you constitute yourself as a reporter of your experience? I don't feel that I'm reporting my experience at all . . .

JOHN BERGER

> No, I don't. Because I believe absolutely in experience being shareable. I believe that the imagination is precisely that. It begins very early in childhood. It begins with the identification of a child with a toy, or with an animal. That capacity of empathy is, it seems to me, the first fruit of that social creation, which is imagination. And in general, today, there is a kind of failure of nerve in fiction – what do I mean by that? I mean that . . .

SUSAN SONTAG

(amused)

> Yes, what do you mean by that?!

JOHN BERGER

> Well I mean that most novels, probably, are really now disguised autobiographies. And on the other hand people say, how do you have the right to write about peasants? You're not a peasant! How do you have the right to write about men? You're not a man, or vice-versa . . . And these questions are very current. And the crisis of nerve, the failure of nerve, is that it is not possible to write about what one has not lived, or what one has not seen. But I don't believe that.

SUSAN SONTAG

> You think that's why there's so many novels about professors because—

JOHN BERGER

> Yes, of course!

SUSAN SONTAG

Or about writers?

JOHN BERGER

Yes, obviously! And finally—

SUSAN SONTAG

Don't you think this also has to do with the competition of other modes of storytelling? Because we've gone from the broadest sense of storytelling, the oral storytelling, to the specifically literary model, but after all we have storytelling through movies—

JOHN BERGER

Yes, but there's always a story behind them. I mean the story has to be written first, not necessarily in book form.

SUSAN SONTAG

No, but I'm not saying that. I'm saying: don't you think that a lot of the so-called crisis of storytelling – I think here you're thinking specifically of a crisis, or a sense of incertitude, or a limitation of ambitions, let's say, among most fiction writers. We're talking about the writers of so-called novels and stories. But a movie director, who is often, at least in Europe, the same person as the author of the script doesn't think that he or she cannot make a movie about some milieu or environment which he or she doesn't share. Movies are about lots of different things . . .

JOHN BERGER

(acquiescing)

Yes!

SUSAN SONTAG
> Movies are about more different things perhaps – I'm talking about serious movies, movies we admire and we like – than fiction is. Why should the fiction writers be demoralised? Why should they feel these sorts of scruples that you're suggesting? I think it's partly because they feel the competition and the success of other modes of storytelling, which have a larger audience. The fact is that written fiction has, proportionally, a smaller audience.

JOHN BERGER
> I think something different. I mean, I think that the novelist is somebody who says: come and I'm going to show you what is happening inside that private house, that private heart! And finally, the novel, which is a very small period of the millennia of storytelling, is about the private and the privileged. I mean, there's no reason— When I say that it's not that I'm denigrating novels, but I think that is at the heart of its form. And actually, what happens there is no longer very important in the world.

SUSAN SONTAG
> Oh, I couldn't disagree with you more! I mean, first of all, we have all the tradition of nineteenth-century novel writings—

JOHN BERGER
(interrupting her)
> It was good then, very important!

SUSAN SONTAG

> But I think it's important now! I mean, I don't think Zola, or Balzac, or Dickens are saying, come I will show you the private as opposed to the public. I think it's precisely that they thought that the private and the public were interrelated, in a sense that they wouldn't anymore—

JOHN BERGER

(interrupting her)

> And they were then!

SUSAN SONTAG

> I think they still are. I mean human nature hasn't changed.

JOHN BERGER

> No, but the capacity of choices has changed. Novels are about choices, stories are often about being up against it. Where there's almost no choice, except how do you react to that, with courage, with cunning, with caution – those sorts of choices. But those big choices and their consequences, which is the theme of so, so much in novels, those choices are no longer open to most people.

SUSAN SONTAG

> I don't believe that. I never thought I would come out as a great defender of the modern age, but I don't believe that people have fewer choices now. I think, in many senses, they have much larger choices. One could say that their sense of choice has been devalued, precisely by being so expanded, as perhaps our sense of art has been devalued by the

very multiplicity of art products that we're surrounded with through various means of reproduction and dissemination and diffusion of art. But I don't think we have fewer choices.

JOHN BERGER

No . . .

SUSAN SONTAG

I think we are precisely suffering from a kind of crisis of imagination, or crisis of nerve. But I don't think it's because we're more unfree now than we were, or we don't make choices about our lives . . .

JOHN BERGER

Who is 'we', there? That's the important question. Yes, we are more free but, well . . .

SUSAN SONTAG

I think more people are free. I think the vast majority of people of course are not free in the sense that we, in this part of the world, are free. But I think more people are free . . . John, we're going to go on talking about this for many years I'm sure, but now alas we have to stop.

(to the audience)

Good night.

SUSAN SONTAG

Send me Something

Letters, 1975–98

Correspondence from John Berger's personal archives, Quincy, and Susan Sontag's papers and personal library, Charles E. Young Research Library, Department of Special Collections, UCLA.

[Missing: letter from John Berger dated 27 November 1974]

['Send her Manhattan' quoted]

31 rue de la Faisanderie
Paris XVI

21 March 1975

>Dear John,
>
>You won't perhaps be surprised to learn that your letter dated Nov. 27, 1974 arrived today. At last, it arrived.
>
>Are the gods against our seeing each other again? Alas, I leave in two days for New York (I've been in Paris since Christmas), but I'll be back in Paris at the end of May. American address: 340 Riverside Drive, New York, NY 10025. French address as above.
>
>Yes, I did get the poetry books and thank you very much.
>
>No word from the BBC about <u>Promised Lands</u>, though they still have the print (I think). Could you drop them (him? her?) a note and jog them a little. I'm afraid they've just forgotten to make a decision.
>
>I often think of you; send messages to you via obscure English or Swiss people who claim to know you; and wish we could see each other again. Do you think that might be possible in June or later in the summer? I'll be mostly in Paris, but I'll come to see you – train? – if you're avoiding this moribund metropolis.
>
>I miss you and send love—
>Susan

P.S. I re-read G a few weeks ago and liked and admired it even more (if possible) this time.

P.P.S. Do send me a few lines to New York to let me know you got this. I'm worried that you may no longer be at this address. And the mail . . .

Send to Manhattan.

31, rue de la Faisanderie
Paris XVI

21 March 1975

Dear John

You won't perhaps be surprised to learn that your letter dated Nov. 27, 1974 arrived today. At least, it arrived.

Are the gods against our seeing each other again? Alas, I leave in two days for New York (I've been in Paris since Christmas), but I'll be back in Paris at the end of May. ~~New York~~ American address: 340 Riverside Drive, New York, New York 10025. French address as above.

Yes, I did get the poetry books and thank you very much.

No word from the BBC about Promised Lands, though they still have the print (I think). Could you drop them (him? her?) a note and jog them a little. I'm afraid they've just forgotten to make a decision.

I often think of you; send messages to you via obscure English or Swiss people who claim to know you; and wish we could see each other again. Do you think that might be possible in June or later in the summer? I'll be mostly in Paris, but I'll come to see you — train? — if you're avoiding this moribund metropolis.

I miss you and send love

Susan

P.S. I re-read G a few weeks ago and liked and admired it even more ('if possible) this time.

P.P.S. Do send me a few lines to New York to let me know you got this. I'm worried that you may no longer be at this address. And the mail...

Chez Mme Coudurier
Cloiset
Mieussy, France 74

12 Aug. 75

>Dear Susan,
>
>I wonder whether Penguins ever have sent you, as I asked them to, the book on migrant workers.
>
>I wonder where you are and why <u>you haven't sent me anything you write</u>? No other reader will follow you more closely than I. I breathe down your neck!
>
>The immediate reason for writing is this. You know the magazine <u>Time Out</u> in London? It's the only "culture" paper read by the young in large numbers. And it has quite a good political record. Literary editor is an American from New York – called Matt Hoffman. I like him. He did an interview with me which I enclose – because it may give you an idea about how he works. He is very anxious to do an interview with you. And I said I'd ask you on his behalf. I don't want to try to persuade you. I'd just say: if you wanted to say something to London – it's a good place, and Matt H. would not trick you in my way. And then it's up to you.
>
>I send you my love,
>Send me something,
>John

[Enclosed: copy from *Time Out*, May 30–June 5, 1975, pages 10–11]

[Postmark: 2-8-1976]

Cloiset
Mieussy
France 74

>Dear Susan,
>
>Welcome back to your Paris quiet and finish the fifth essay!
>
>I just wanted to tell you what a great pleasure and inspiration you were to us both. The content of our 24 hours was such that now it seems far too short but nevertheless the equivalent of about 72 hours!
>
>I read your interview again and admire your precision and courage. What you say there about the past is very important. And the way that you relate art to it. (Interesting theme: the way that stories are inevitably – but often, often, more than is 'necessary' – set in the past. Hence, one of the problematics of science fiction, and the strange thug one always feels when reading it within past and future – it is nearly always the past disguised as the future).
>
>After your interview this is a long essay on Kracauer. I've read one book on film by him, that's all. The essay makes his book on history sound perhaps interesting. Do you know it? Do you think it's still findable in New York?
>
>I want to send a book to David, back with you in September. Does he read French? Does he read poetry? That will help me choose.
>
>What you said about the stories was of

immense help. And will, I think, speed up considerably the otherwise so slow process of opening out and extension. And one day I'll write the story of the horse for you.

Please send me things. And please ask me when you need something I can offer. No matter what.

With my love,
John

Sometime can you send me a photocopy of the text of my piece about Goya? (Pictures unnecessary). Art Forum in N.Y. have asked me to send something.

[Sun drawing]

Susan,
The warmth you give is strong – like the sun. You give so fully. I feel no cancer can finally harm you. But know that in my thoughts I try to help you in your struggle – you have a new friend whose concern and love are very real. Thank you for being you.

B. [Beverly]

12 Aug 75.

Chez Mlle ‑ Coudurier
Cloiset
Mieussy. France 74.
—·

Dear Susan —

I wonder whether Penguins have sent you, as I asked them to, the book on migrant workers.

I wonder where you are and why you never send me anything you write? No other reader will follow you more closely than I. I breathe down your neck!

The immediate reason for writing is this. You know the magazine Time Out in London? It's the only "culture" paper read by the young in large numbers. And it has quite a good political record. Their literary editor is an American from New York — called Matt Hoffman. I like him. He did an interview with me which I enclose — because it may give you an idea about how he works. He is very anxious to do an interview with you. And I said I'd ask you on his behalf. I don't want to try to persuade you. I'd just say: if you wanted to say something to London — it's a good place, and Matt. H. would

not push you in any way. And
then it's up to you.

I send you my love
send me something

John.

Susan Sontag
Chez Nicole Stéphane
31 Rue de Faisanderie
PARIS 16ᵉ

Cloiset
Mieussy
France 74.

Dear Susan,

Welcome back to your Paris quiet and finish the fifth essay!

I just wanted to tell you what a great pleasure and inspiration you were to us both. The content of our 24 hrs was sure too now it seems far too short but nonetheless the equivalent of about 72 hours!

I read your interview again and admire your precision and courage. What you say there about the past is very important. And the way that you relate art to it. (Interesting there: the way that stories are inevitably — but often, often, more than is 'necessary' — set in the past. Hence, one of the problematics of science fiction, and the strange tug one always feels when reading it between past and future — it is nearly always the past <u>disguised</u> as the future.)

After your interview this is a long essay on <u>Kracauer</u>. I've read one book on film by him, that's all. The essay makes his book on history sound perhaps interesting. Do you know it? Do you think it's still findable in New York?

I want to send a book to David, back with you in September. Does he read French? Does he read poetry? That will help me chose.

What you said about the stories was of immense help. And will, I think, speed up considerably the otherwise so slow process of opening out and extension. And one day I'll write the story of the horse for <u>you</u>.

Please send me things. And please ask me whenever you need something I can offer. No matter what.

        With my love
            John.

Sometime can you send me a photocopy of the text of my piece about Sogn? (pictures unnecessary). Art Forum in N.Y. have asked me to send something.

Susan,
The warmth you give is strong — like the sun. You give so fully. I feel no cancer can finally harm you. But know that in my thoughts I try to help you in your struggle — you have a new friend whose concern and love are very real. Thank you for being you. B.

14/2/78

Cloiset
Mieussy
France 74

>Dearest Susan,
>
>Valentine's day and so I send you this! Anyway, all months of the year I love you! You have written a marvellous and very important book.
>
>This review which I spent much time on – but is inadequate to your achievement – I hope to publish full length in the New Left Review and, in a shortened version, in *Seven Days*, New York. Is that a good idea?
>
>Please get the N.Y.R. [New York Review] of Books to send me your essays on illness. Their fame has reached here, but not copies.
>
>I wonder how you are. I long to see you. How?
>I admire and embrace you – very hard,
>John
>
>P.S. If you see Roger Strauss, please tell him I'm going to write to him. The snow is so high.

[Enclosed: 'Susan Sontag and the Practice of Photography', typescript, handwritten title on first page, pages 1–15]

19/3/78

Mieussy
France 74

> Dear Susan,
> The last four pages of the piece I sent you were poor. Re-reading them I was ashamed. Here they are re-written and better thought. Yesterday your N.Y.B.R. [New York Review of Books] essays arrived and I am just about to read them.
> With my love
> As always,
> John

[Enclosed: 'Susan Sontag and the Practice of Photography', typescript, corrected pages 12–15, first published 7 April 1978 as 'Photography: God of the Instant', *Seven Days*, and revised as 'Ways of Remembering', *Camerawork*, 10 July 1978]

[Postmark: Mieussy, 25-7-1978]

>Dearest Susan,
>>Come and see us. With my love as always—
>>John

[Handwritten on the 1st of 5 enclosed items: 'Photography and Memory' 1, 2 & 3 and 'Alternative Photography' 1 & 2, typescript and marked-up proof stage for publication in *New Society*, August 1978]

14/2/78.

Cloiset
Mieussy
France 74
E.

Dearest Susan,

Valentine's day and so I send you this! Anyway all months of the year I love you! You have written a marvelous and very important book.

This review which I spent much time on — but is inadequate to your achievement — I hope to publish full length in the New Left Review, and, in a shortened version, in Seven Days, New York. Is that a good idea?

Please get the N.Y.R of Books. to send me your — essays on illness. Their fame has reached here, but not copies.

I wonder how you are. I long to see you. How? I admire and embrace you — very hard John.

P.S. If you see Roger Straus, please tell him I'm going to write to him. The snow is so high.

19/3/78.   Micussy
                                   France 74.

Dear Susan,
  The last four pages of the piece I sent you were poor. Re-reading them I was ashamed. Here they are re-written and better thought. Yesterday your N.Y.B.R. essays I received and I am just about to read them.
            with my love
                  as always
                      John.

Susan Sontag.
Chez Nicole Stéphane.
31 Rue de la Faisanderie
PARIS 16ᵉ.

New Society—Photography and memory—1

Arts in society
Photography and memory
John Berger

I want in two articles to discuss certain aspects of the past uses and the possible future uses of photography. All my remarks are a response to Susan Sontag's new book, *On Photography* (Allen Lane £5.50). Because in these essays Susan Sontag lays down the basis for a theory of the use of photographs—with all the social, historical and ideological practices which that implies—her book can claim to be the most original and important work yet written on the subject. The quotations I will use are from her text. The thoughts are sometimes my own, but all originate in the experience of reading her essays.

The camera was invented by Fox Talbot in 1839. Within a mere 30 years of its invention as a gadget for an elite, photography was being used for police filing, war reporting, military reconnaissance, pornography, encyclopedic documentation, family albums, postcards, anthropological records (often, as with the Indians in the United States accompanied by genocide), sentimental moralising, inquisitive probing—the wrongly named "candid camera", aesthetic effects, news reporting and formal portraiture. The first cheap popular camera was put on the market, a little later, in 1888. The speed with which the possible uses of photography were seized upon is surely an indication of photography's profound, central applicability to industrial capitalism. Marx came of age the year of the camera's invention.

[Typewritten copy]

207 E. 17th St.
New York, N.Y. 10003

February 24, 1980

>Dear Mr. Engelhardt:
>
>As you probably know, I am a great admirer of John Berger's work, and I hope that finally, because Pantheon has the good fortune to have become his publisher, he will be recognized for the superb and original writer that he is. I agree with you that his book on Picasso is marvellous, and I'm very glad that he has decided to reprint some of the wonderful short essays he's been publishing in New Society. I only wish he had chosen to reprint more of them.
>
>Although I rarely give quotes for books, I would be glad to give one for John Berger. That, however, is not what you are asking me to do. You are suggesting that I review the book; it is not likely that I will be able to do this, not because Mr. Berger has written about me, but because I have stopped writing essays for a while, and am working on a novel. But let me repeat, I want to support Mr. Berger's work in every way I can. You are right to think that I feel my own ideas and perceptions and questions are very close to his.
>
>Yours,

[Hand-signed]

>Susan Sontag
>
>P.S. Didn't Pantheon publish a book called American Photographs? Could you send me a copy? Many thanks.

207 E. 17th St.
New York, N.Y. 10003

February 24, 1980

Dear Mr. Engelhardt:

As you probably know, I am a great admirer of John Berger's work, and I hope that finally, because Pantheon has the good fortune to have become his publisher, he will be recognized for the superb and original writer that he is. I agree with you that his book on Picasso is marvelous, and I'm very glad that he has decided to reprint some of the wonderful short essays he's been publishing in New Society. I only wish he had chosen to reprint more of them.

Although I rarely give quotes for books, I would be glad to give one for John Berger. That, however, is not what you are asking me to do. You are suggesting that I review the book; it is not likely that I will be able to do this, not because Mr. Berger has written about me, but because I have stopped writing essays for a while, and am working on a novel. But let me repeat, I want to support Mr. Berger's work in every way I can. You are right to think that I feel my own ideas and perceptions and questions are very close to his.

Yours,

Susan Sontag

P.S. Didn't Pantheon publish a book called American Photographs? Could you send me a copy? Many thanks.

[Neither place nor date, likely: London, 1981]

John,

What impressed me so much the first time I read about what you call a 'language of appearances' – was that I had been trying to make the wrong distinction – between 'image' and 'concept' – and your word suggested the philosophical distinction between appearance and essence, a more useful one (for distinguishing photographic images from poetic or painted images). Now you make further refinements: 'appearances' are not positivistic, factual givens but a 'half-language' that needs completion by an actively receptive subject (very Benjaminian!) in the act of storytelling. What you say about photograph's subversive tending vis a vis history, as arresting time, also seems right.

I am worried only at two points: one is the discussion of these 'quotations' as particular expressions of the general . . . especially the Hegel analogy. Here the distinction between appearances and concept is in danger of being lost, and that would be a mistake. Or – one is caught in a kind of hermeneutics of 'experiences' as empathy – whereas the very idea of a photograph is excited by the tension because the inside of a human experience is reached solely externally by obscuring the external surfaces of objects photographed. How does the 'general' actually differ in a photograph from Hegel's concept? Certainly one of the greatest ambiguities of photographs is its positing and undermining the distinction between subject and object – without ever moving to a level of (abstract) identity.

The other point – what would be the 'narrative form' of photographs. This of course depends on John's photographs – so I really am not in a position to comment. Certainly what you say about the reciprocity of juxtaposed images which distinguishes photography – montage from film – montage . . . is striking. But is it really comparable to memory-images? Photographic montage may look the same as memory images – but they are really an immersion . . . I just am not clear on this – you do say that the montage allows the appropriation of the images by reflection. I can follow you here, but I don't quite see it.

Reading this gets my excitement up again for the Cretan project. I really can't wait to send it to you – some of it you are sure to like . . .

John, it was a delight to see you and Beverly – and Yves and your mother and Nashville – last night. I'm so glad I caught you in town.

Enclosed is the information on the Cornell proposal. I for one would be delighted if you could come.

I got a confirmed seat at standby price from Olympic airways to fly to Athens and to Crete tomorrow, leaving at noon. I'll stay three weeks.

My love to you all. Have a good drive home.
Susan

[Enclosed information not found]

John –

What impressed me so much the first time I read about
what you call a "language of ~~images~~ appearances" – was that I had been trying to
make the wrong distinction – between "image" and "concept" –
and your usual suggested the philosophical distinction between appearance
and essence, a more useful one (for distinguishing photographic images from
pure or ~~active~~ painted images) Now you make a further refinements:
"appearances" are not possibilities, factural "givens" but a "half-language"
that needs completion by an actively receptive subject (very
Benjaminian!) via the act of history. What you say about photographs'
subversive tendency vis a vis history, as arresting time, also seems right.

I am worried only at two points: one is the discussion of these
"quotations" as particular expressions of the general – especially the
Hegel ~~you~~ analogy. Here the distinction between appearance and
concept is in danger of being lost, and that would be a mistake.
Or – one is caught in a kind of hermeneutics of "experience" as
sympathy – whereas the very idea of a photograph is excited by the tension ~~between~~ because
the inside of ~~an~~ a human experience is reached solely externally
~~by observing~~ the external surfaces of
~~the~~ objects photographed. How does the "general" actually
differ in a photograph from Hegel's concept? Certainly one of the
greatest ambiguities of photographs is its positing and undermining
the distinction between subject and object – without ever moving
to a level of (abstract) identity.

The ~~three~~ other point – what would be the "narrative form" of
photographs. This of course depends on John's

photographies - so I really am not in a position to comment.
Certainly what you say about the reciprocity of juxtaposed
images which distinguishes photography - montage from
film - montage ... is striking. But is it really comparable
to memory images? ~~Photomas~~ Photographic montage may look the same as memory
images - but they are really ~~of~~ an inversion .... I just
am not clear on this - you do say that montage allows the
~~appropriation~~ of the images by reflection. I can follow you here,
but I don't quite ~~see~~ it.

Reading this sets my excitement up again for the Cretan
project. I really can't wait to send it to you - some of it you are
sure to like ....

John, it was a delight to see you and Beverley —
and Yves and your mother and Nashville — last night.
I'm so glad I caught you in town.

Enclosed is the information on the Cornell proposal.
I for one would be delighted if you could come.

I got a confirmed seat at standby price from Olympic
airways to fly to Athens + on to Crete tomorrow, leaving at
noon. I'll stay three weeks. Have a good drive home —
My love to you all.

Susan

['Telephone' quoted]

31 May, 1982

> Dear John,
>
> For a while now I've been imagining coming to see you and bringing with me word (your own copy?) of Benjamin's <u>Passagenarbeit</u> and showing you some of my <u>Tour-guide to Modern Experience</u>, the project that takes me to Crete, which we talked about together in London a year ago.
>
> I have been staying in Paris. I have a grant for next year (at Cornell) to work on the <u>Passagenarbeit</u>, and possibly for another year, a Humboldt to do same in Germany. (I am here to help my French and working at the Bibliothèque national during a semester's leaves). The <u>Passagenarbeit</u> was supposed to have been out early this year. Now it is scheduled to appear <u>at</u> the Suhrkamp Verlag celebration of Benjamin's 90th Birthday, July 1–3 (speeches by Löwenthal, Tiedemann, etc.).
>
> On 9th July I am supposed to be in Crete for an ethnology conference.
>
> Now here's my thought: I will be leaving Frankfurt July 3rd or 4th. I have 5 days before I have to be in Crete. Allowing 3 days for overland travel, that still leaves 2 for stopping off to see you (4th–6th, or 5th–7th), I don't know any of the travel-feasibility details, but thought I would at least write and see if it's at all a possibility for you at your end. Will you all be up way on top of the mountain with the cows? I remember talk of

summers really far out of reach.

If you are in reach, but short on time, we could meet in Geneva for a meal and a talk (then I would go on and spend a night or 2 with a friend in Florence). Either that, or my coming to Mieussy is possible, I think, for me to manage.

We could discuss too at that time the still very alive offer to bring you to Cornell next fall.

Or, are you coming to Paris? I could put you and Beverly up easily (perhaps Eve [Yves] too) and would love to see you.

I will most likely stay in Crete for July (am giving up my apartment here). If I decide after I see the Passagenarbeit that another month at the Bibliothèque nationale would really be helpful, I might try to come back here in August and stay. But at the present my reservation is to fly Paris–New York on August 4th.

I am teaching in the fall 'Cultural History as a Subversive Activity' and we are reading Adorno on Wagner, Benjamin on Baudelaire, Barthes on Balzac, Rich on the Brontës and Berger on Picasso. I'm looking forward to it.

Marc Raskin was here when I came; Susan George has been a pleasure to see, Dick Barnet is coming to town this weekend. Paris is fast and hard, zipping here & there on the metro, and getting your brain-nerves titillated in the most outrageously promises-without-delivery manner.

I like my Crete book. It keeps changing and I think getting better.

It was truly a pleasure to see you and Beverly in London last year. I do hope we can manage to again this year.

My love to her, and to you,
Susan

Buch-Horss
9, rue Fenoux
15eme Paris
Tel: 250.8117.

P.S. Do you want a copy of the Passagenarbeit if I come? I expect it to be expensive and heavy (several volumes, maybe 70–100) but would be glad to provide delivery.

S.

Telephone.   31 aug, 1982

Dear John,

For a while now I've been imagining coming to see you and bringing with me a word (your own copy?) of Benjamin's *Passagenarbeit*, and showing you some of my Roughguide Tour-Guide to Modern Experience, the project that takes me to Crete, which we talked about together in London a year ago.

I have been staying in Paris. I have a grant for next year (at Cornell) to work on the Passagenarbeit, and possibly, in another year, a Humboldt to do same in Germany. (I am here to help my French and working at the Bibliothèque nationale doing a semester's leave). The Passagenarbeit was supposed to have been out early this year, now it is scheduled to appear at the Suhrkamp Verlag celebration of Benjamin's 90ᵗʰ birthday, July 1-3 (speeches by Lowenthal, Tiedemann, etc.)

On 9ᵗʰ July I am supposed to be in Crete for an ethnology conference.

Now here's my thought. I will be leaving Frankfurt July 3rd or 4ᵗʰ. I have 5 days before I have to be in Crete. Allowing 3 days for overland travel, that still leaves 2 for stopping off to see you. (4ᵗʰ-6ᵗʰ, or 5ᵗʰ-7ᵗʰ). I don't know any of the travel-feasibility details, but thought I would at least write and see if it is at all a possibility for you at your end. Will you all be up way on top of the mountains with the cows? I remember talk of summers really far out of reach.

If you are in reach, but short on time, we could meet in Geneva for a meal and a talk (then I would go on and spend a night or 2 with a friend in Florence). Either that, or my coming to visit you is possible, I think, for me to manage. We could discuss two at that time the still very alive offer to bring you to Cornell next fall.

Or, are you coming to Paris? I could put you and Beverly up easily (perhaps Eve too) and would love to see you.

I will most likely stay in Crete for July (I am giving up my apartment here). If I decide after I see the Passagenarbeit that another month at the Bibliothèque nationale would really be helpful, I might try to come back here in August and stay. But at present my reservation is to fly Paris — New York on August 4th.

I am teaching in the fall "Cultural History as a Subversive Activity" and we are reading Adorno on Wagner, Benjamin on Baudelaire, Barthes on Balzac, Rich on the Brontës and Berger on Picasso. I'm looking forward to it.

Marc Raskin was here when I came, Susan George has been a pleasure to see, Dick Barnet is coming to town this weekend. Paris is fast and hard, zipping here + there on the metro, and getting your brain-nerves titillated in the most outrageously promises-without-delivery manner.

I like my Crete book. It keeps changing and I think getting better.

It was truly a pleasure to see you and Beverly in London last year. I do hope we can manage it again this year.
My love to her, and to you.

Susan

Buck-Morss
9, rue Fenoux
15ème Paris
tel. 250.8117.

P.S. Do you want a copy of the Passagenarbeit if I come? I expect it to be expensive and heavy (several volumes, maybe 70-$100) but would be glad to provide delivery
S.

[Postmark: Meaux, 10-02-1983]

8/2/83

Quincy Mieussy
France 74440

> My dear Susan,
>
> For me it was a real pleasure to spend those few hours with you! – 'retakes' notwithstanding! Let it not be too long before we meet again.
>
> The T.L.S. [*Times Literary Supplement*] hesitated about publishing our conversation and so I was glad to be able to say 'why not drop it?'. And I think Udi's [Eichler] honour was saved.
>
> As for the programme, when I saw it I was convinced that it has a quality (at least for European Television) of innovation. The quality of two people really listening to each other. Others could listen in to them listening! Whether or not the others went on listening or switched off is, I think, only a secondary question. Even those who switched off (perhaps not so many?) switched off something different. Whatever we may have been feeling or thinking inside, we produced something which was not addressed to the camera, and all that that camera normally organises and arranges. It was very cool – (toward the screen) and at the same time warm and involved as between us. And of that I think we can be proud.
>
> I hope it went well for you in Rome and that you weren't too tired.
>
> Two days later I got a phone-call from my

nineteen-year-old son Jacob in New York. He's studying at the New York University film school. He's very clever, very funny and he cares a lot. Sometimes I think he's <u>my</u> father! He wonders whether he could meet you for half an hour. He wants to ask you for help (recommendation) about a scholarship he hopes to get for next year. I told him you didn't know his work, and I did not give him your telephone number. Because I don't think he, I, or anybody should impose anything on you. Probably you don't know me well enough to know that I'm never a father with capital F? If Jacob was a pastry-maker and enjoyed it, I'd be more than happy. So if I say that his work is in fact very serious, I don't think I'm being prejudiced. He surprises me.

Anyway, should it interest you to see him (and <u>please</u> do not let it be a corvée), I suggest that you contact him, for then it could be at your convenience. Jacob Berger, Room 1401 Brittany House, 55 East 10th St. Tel. 212 420 8554.

I hope that the most surprising and fantastic (in the sense of our conversation) spoken words go on coming into your head, forcing you to find the speakers! Take care, continue as you are—

With love,
John

Cornell University
The Society for the Humanities
Andrew D. White House
27 East Avenue, Ithaca, New York 14853

March 15, 1983

Dear John,

Since December I have been studying Benjamin's Passagen-Werk. I keep thinking of you and of your interests, and I believe the Passagen-Werk crosses your work in interesting ways, interesting because of the political questions that emerge at the crossings.

One of the themes in the book is world's exhibitions as a phantasmagoria of commodities. It is no accident, I believe, that the Paris Benjamin knew in 1931 and 1937 had large world's expositions. It is also politically relevant that Paris will have another in 1989, celebrating the bicentennial of the French (bourgeois) Revolution.

There ought to be a film, grounded in Benjamin's book, in time to counter this brand new phantasmagoria which (like the world's Expositions of 1867 and 1937) comes at the brink of war.

You ought to make that film.

I will be in Paris for the Benjamin conference June 26–30. I think you have been invited. If you aren't coming, is there any chance we could meet in Europe before/after the conference? I would really like to talk with you about this. Meanwhile, I have some written pieces I could send you.

Warmest regards,
Susan

Personal.

PAR AVION

SCEAUX PRINCIPAL
10-02-83 17H
92330

RÉPUBLIQUE FRANÇAISE
003,90
POSTES
G1 PC72071

Susan Sontag.
~~<strikethrough>~~
207 East 17ᵗʰ St.
New York.
N.Y.

États-Unis.

8/3/83.

Quincy
Mieussy
France
74440

My dear Susan — for me it was a real pleasure to spend those few hours with you — "retakes" notwithstanding! Let it not be too long before we meet again.

The T.L.S. hesitated about publishing our conversations, and so I was glad to be able to say — "Why not drop it?". And I think Ulis' honour was saved.

As for the programme, when I saw it I was convinced that "it" had a quality (at least for European Television) of innovation. The quality of two people really listening to each other. Others could listen in to them listening! Whether or not the others want on listening or switched off is, I think, only a secondary question. Even those who switched off (perhaps not so many?) switched off something different. Whatever we may have been feeling or thinking inside, we produced something which was not addressed to the camera, and all that that camera normally organises and arranges. It was very cool —(towards the screen) and at the same time warm and involved as between us. And of that I think we can be proud.

I hope it went well for you in Rome, and that you weren't too tired.

Two days later I got a phone-call from my 19 year old son Jacob in New York. He's studying at the New York University film school. He's very clever, very funny and he cares a lot. Sometimes I think he's my father! He wonders whether he could meet you for half an hour. He wants to ask you for help (recommendation) about a scholarship he hopes to get for next year. I told him you did'nt know his work, and I did not give him your telephone number. Because I don't think he, I, or anybody should impose anything on you. Probably you dont know me well enough to know that I'm never a father with a capital F.? If Jacob was a pastry-maker and enjoyed it, I'd be more than happy. So if I say that his work is in fact very serious, I dont think I'm being prejudiced. He surprises me.

Anyway, should it interest you to see him (but please do not let it be a corvée), I suggest that you contact him, for then it could be at your convenience. Jacob Burger, Room 1401 Brittany House, 55 East 10th St. Tel. 212 420 8554.

I hope that the most surprising and fantastic (in the sense of our conversations) spoken words go on coming into your head, forcing you to find the speakers! Take care, continue as you are —

with my love
John

CORNELL UNIVERSITY
THE SOCIETY FOR THE HUMANITIES
ANDREW D. WHITE HOUSE
27 EAST AVENUE, ITHACA, NEW YORK 14853

Personal

607-256-4725 Fellows
607-256-4086 Director

March 15, 1983

Dear John,

Since December I have been studying Benjamin's *Passagen-Werk*. I keep thinking of you and of your interests, and I believe the *Passagen-Werk* crosses your work in interesting ways, interesting because of the political questions that emerge at the crossings.

One of the themes in the book is world's exhibitions as a phantasmagoria of commodities. It is no accident, I believe, that the Paris Benjamin knew in 1931 and 1937 had large world's Expositions. It is also politically relevant that Paris will have another in 1989, celebrating the bicentennial of the French (bourgeois) revolution.

There ought to be a film, grounded in Benjamin's book, in time to counter this brand new phantasmagoria which (like the world's Expositions of 1867 and 1937) comes at the brink of war.

You ought to make that film.

I will be in Paris for the Benjamin conference June 26-30. I think you have been invited. If you aren't coming, is there any chance we could meet in Europe before/after the conference? I would really like to talk with you about this. Meanwhile, I have some written pieces I could send you.

Warmest regards,
Susan

[Typewritten original]

36 King Street
New York, NY 10014

July 16, 1990

Dearest John,

I regret so much that we've not seen each other in the last few years. I spend less time in Paris than I used to and you have, understandably, little interest in coming to New York . . .

My great friend and exemplary publisher, Roger Straus, tells me that he has reason to hope that he will be able to publish you from now on. I assume this has something to do with the ignominious devolution of Pantheon.

I've always hoped that you could be published by Farrar, Straus & Giroux. With all due respect to Andre Schiffrin and what he was able to do with Pantheon, I think Farrar, Straus & Giroux has been the all-around best literary publisher in America all these years. You'll be very pleased by the way they work and the care they take – if that's the decision you make.

In a couple of days I'm leaving for Berlin. I have been given an apartment there for three months and I hope to finish the novel I've been working on – all too intermittently – for the last two years. I doubt if you see The New Yorker often, so I enclose a few things that I've published there in the last few years, which are probably the best things I've done recently.

I do hope we will see each other soon. I think of

you often and was so touched by the wine you sent me, via David Hermann, in Paris. Please let me hear from you soon. I send much, much love—
 Susan

[Enclosed items not found, likely: 'The Case of Machado de Assis', *The New Yorker*, April 29, 1990; 'Pilgrimage, Tea with Thomas Mann', *The New Yorker*, December 14, 1987; 'The Way we Live Now', *The New Yorker*, November 16, 1986; 'The Letter Scene', *The New Yorker*, August 10, 1986]

1/8/90

Tel 50 43 03 36
Quincy
Mieussy
74440
France

>Dearest Susan,
>
>I wonder whether this letter will find you in Berlin – and of course writing it I'm in the world of letters you write about so beautifully – without hiding and without stripping – like the heart is, but little else in this world. Thank you for sending me all those pages – they brought you very close. We are very different but we come from the same place – and what you write now takes me back there. There was Merrill and you and me. It's your heart and the way you write that does it – so I too was in southern California!
>
>Where I never was at the appropriate time was New York – so when Pantheon were mugged, the only thing I could do (on the advice of my friends in Pantheon) was to put myself into Andrew Wylie's hands. (He's not your agent too?) I like him because he's like an airline pilot – and doesn't (like so many agents) carry on as if he were Erich Auerbach! He considered Farrow Strauss very seriously – but the problem was getting my books away from Pantheon. (The third book of the trilogy was published without a sound of response or a splash. I wonder even if they sent you a copy, as I asked.) It looks as though he's now settling for a

"Random House deal" with Vintage. On this condition Pantheon will open their mouth and let the rabbits – fur a bit wet – drop out, so they can be picked up and put in another hutch. I'm trying to remember how to write the next book, the trilogy being finished.

In Berlin I know a painter whom I like very much. Very good painter. Forests. Latter day abstract expressionist. Lives in a hut in one of his paintings and reads. (!) His name is Schmidt. Werner. He speaks English. His telephone is 30 34 12 743. You are a star in Berlin of course, everyone will want to see you. But if you want to go to a forest, phone Werner and tell him I gave you his number . . .

Of course I would love to see you – in any year from 1947 onwards – and any place.

Take care, dearest Susan,
Much much love,
John

Sontag

36 King Street
New York, NY 10014

July 16, 1990

Dearest John,

I regret so much that we've not seen each other in the last few years. I spend less time in Paris than I used to and you have, understandably, little interest in coming to New York....

My great friend and exemplary publisher, Roger Straus, tells me that he has reason to hope that he will be able to publish you from now on. I assume this has something to do with the ignominious devolution of Pantheon.

I've always hoped that you could be published by Farrar, Straus & Giroux. With all due respect to Andre Schiffrin and what he was able to do with Pantheon, I think Farrar, Straus & Giroux has been the all-around best literary publisher in America all these years. You'll be very pleased by the way they work and the care they take---if that's the decision you make.

In a couple of days I'm leaving for Berlin. I have been given an apartment there for three months and I hope to finish the novel I've been working on---all too intermittently---for the last two years. I doubt if you see The New Yorker often, so I enclose a few things that I've published there in the last few years, which are probably the best things I've done recently.

I do hope we will see each other soon. I think of you often and was so touched by the wine you sent me, via David Hermann, in Paris. Please let me hear from you soon. I send much, much love.

Susan

Please Forward
PAR AVION

Susan Sontag
36 King St.
New York.
N.Y. 10014.
Etats-Unis.

1/8/90 -.

Tel 50 43 03 36 Quincy
Mieussy
74440
France.

'inventoried'

Dearest Susan —

I wonder whether this letter will find you in Berlin — and of course writing it I'm in the world of letters you write about so beautifully — without hiding and without skipping — like the heart is, but little else in this world. Thank you for sending me all those pages — they brought you very close. We are very different but we came from the same place — and what you so write now takes me back there. There was Merrill and you and me. It's your heart and the way you write that does it — so I too was in southern California!

Where I never was at the appropriate time was New York — so when Pantheon were mugged, the only thing I could do (on the advice of my friends in Pantheon) was to put myself into Andrew Wylie's hand (He's not your agent too?) I like him because he's like an airline pilot — ad doesn't (like so many agents) carry on as if he were Erich Auerbach. He considered Farrar Strauss very serious — but the problem was getting my book away from Pantheon. (The third book of the trilogy was published without a sound of response or a splash. I wonder now if they sent you a copy, is I asked.) It looks as though he's now settling for a "Random House deal" with Vintage. On this condition Pantheon will open their mouth and let the rabbits — fur a bit wet — drop out, so they can be picked up ad put in another hutch. I'm trying to remember how to write the next book, the trilogy being finished.

In Berlin I know a painter

2.

whom I like very much. Very good painter. Forests. Latter day abstract, expressionist. Lives in a hut in one of his paintings ad reads. (!) His name is Schmidt. Werner. He speaks English. His telephone is 30 34 12 743. You are a star in Berlin of course, everyone will want to see you. But if you want to go to a forest, phone Werner ad tell him I gave you his number ...

Of course I would love to see you — in any year from 1947 onwards — ad any place.

Take care, dearest Susan,
much much love

John.

[Typewritten original]

JOHN BERGER
Quincy, Mieussy,
74440 TANINGES,
FRANCE
Tel/Fax (33) 450 430 336

18th May 1998

Susan Sontag
Fax 212 627 5002

>Dear Susan,
>
>On a mountain top – so long ago! I hope all goes very well for you.
>
>Through Juan Villoro at La Jordana, we got the message that you would like to see John's text about Marcos (not always directly about the Zapatistas but written more as Open Letters to him . . .).
>
>I would like to send these but Juan has not given us your full postal code. What I have is 470 West 24th Street, NY NY 1001. Can you supply the missing number please?
>
>All the best,

[Hand-signed]

>Beverly
>And love from John.

[Sent again by fax on the 20th, likely with the following items: 'The Heron who Carried a Message for the Eagle and the Serpent', typescript, 'Marcos' and '*El Pais* – 27/4/95' quoted, John Berger stamp, 'Something Remains Between the Fingers', copy from *DoubleTake*, Spring 1996 & 'How to Live with Stones', copy from *Los Angeles Times*, January 4, 1998]

JOHN BERGER,
Quincy, Mieussy, 74440 TANINGES, FRANCE
Tel/Fax: (33) 450 430 336
(33) 450 430 336

18th May 1998

Susan Sontag,
Fax: 212 627 5002

Dear Susan,

On a mountain top - so long ago!   I hope all goes very well for you.

Through Juan Villoro at La Jornada.we got the message that you would like to see John's text about Marcos. (not always directly about the Zapatistas but written more as Open Letters to him....)

I would like to send these but Juan has not given us your full postal code. What I have is 470 West 24th Street, NY NY 1001.   Can you supply the missing number please?

All the best,

Beverly.

And love from John.

Between Self & System

IDCA, 1974

Talk by John Berger and Susan Sontag at the IDCA
International Design Conference in Aspen, held on 18 June
1974, ⅛ inch audiocassette from Getty Library, Getty
Research Institute, LA.

between self & system

international design conference in aspen

IDCA program book
June 16-21, 1974

between self & system

International Design Conference in Aspen
P. O. Box 664,
Aspen, Colorado 81611

Address correction requested

In our everyday lives, self and system are generally seen as opposites. That we are the source of creativity and that the world constrains us is a notion that permeates our thinking and governs our attitudes towards doing and changing. It is one of the oldest dictums of design.

Yet it seems clear that such concepts for understanding the relationship Between Self and System are inadequate and may be responsible for the widening gulf between ourselves, our actions and the effect of these on the various systems in which we have to live. Man is neither the independent cause of environment nor does the environment wholly shape the individual. The self and the system each accommodate to and make demands on the other. The arrows go both ways.

The 1974 International Design Conference in Aspen will explore, demonstrate and help formulate concepts of interaction between the self (the designer) and the system (the context in which the designer works); with the focus on this interaction as a fundamental function of change.

Morning Talk

SUSAN SONTAG

(on microphone)

> In keeping with the spirit of the conference, I'm not going to do what I was announced to be about to do . . .

(laughter)

> John Berger and I have been talking yesterday and today, discovered a large area of common concern and common interest and we've decided to share our time both this morning. That is, he's going to participate with me and the time that I have here this morning. We're going to have at a certain point a kind of conversation with each other in front of you. And then I'm going to join him this afternoon in the seminar – I guess you could call it – anyway, the smaller meeting that he's having I believe at two o'clock in – where is it . . . ?

MODERATOR
(distantly)
> Upstairs lounge. Aspen meadows . . .

SUSAN SONTAG
> . . . the upstairs lounge? At the Aspen meadows.

(continuing)
> And that discussion this afternoon will probably be a continuation of the themes that we'll be talking about with you this morning, with an inevitably smaller group because the space is much smaller. And one in which a situation therefore – in which the dialogue can include you as well – and we can respond to questions. So as I say I'm going to talk then for just a few minutes now. And then John will come up and stand next to me and we will continue talking together until lunchtime. And then we'll go on with the conversation this afternoon.
>
> I want to start with a couple of remarks about the title of the conference, which is *Self and System* – and which I suppose everyone who gets up here will be commenting on, or referring to, or using in some way. The main remark that I want to make is about that. I want to invite you to consider that choice of terms, because it's a rather striking one. One could say of course that this dichotomy – these two words, 'self' and 'system' – is a reworking or bringing up to date of a very traditional theme, which used to be called 'individual and society'. And that some of the same ground that is being covered in the meetings, and discussions, and visual material, and lectures, that you were attending during this week is what well might have been grouped under, uh . . . that

amounts to material that might well have been grouped under that older, over-familiar term – set of terms 'individual and society'.

Therefore, one of the first questions that I ask myself is why 'self and systems', rather than 'individual and society'? – apart from, perhaps, the natural impulse to choose a fresher sounding set of terms. Is there something in the pairing of the words 'self' and 'system' that can be said which is not said when one uses the more familiar form of that dichotomy. And I think indeed there is. I think that the term 'self' is a very particular version, a very loaded version of the notion of the individual – or of individuality – and that the notion of 'system' is again a very loaded – ideologically loaded – version of what might have been described. I don't say better described, I simply say more familiarly described as society, or societies, or perhaps even communities – a notion which is not much talked about in this context of talking about systems.

Both the pairing of the notions of self and system carries certain kinds of mechanistic overtones which to me are very striking. When we talk about a society, we have in back of us a whole literature and tradition of thinking which is based on organic – or organistic models. Societies grow, systems are set up. Societies have in the traditional literature of political philosophy most often been compared or treated as comparable to natural organisms. And I'm talking about the whole tradition of political philosophy – Aristotle, Hobbes, Rousseau, Hegel and so forth – compared to the human organism, compared to biological organism, compared to so-called natural units like the family. Whereas to talk about systems is to invoke another set of metaphors. Inevitably terms like 'self' and 'system' are metaphors. They have to be metaphors. The question is what kind of metaphors they are. And the fact that we are using a language which is heavily indebted to mechanistic metaphors I think is an interesting thing to become aware of – and tells us a great deal about the way our concerns are being redirected according to the ideology of this society, and tells us also about the form of our meeting together in Aspen for this week and the kinds of events that are taking place here.

This mechanistic language is a reductive language. 'Self' is a reductive term in relation to the notion of the individual. 'System' is a reductive term with a particular ideological intent with relation to society. If we take for instance the notion of systems we are subliminally carrying into any conversation that we have on that subject the idea that a system consists of parts – as a machine consists of parts – that a system is built or assembled, that it can be dismantled, that one part can be used to replace another, that you can repair it, that parts become exchangeable or interchangeable. We are setting up by this change of language a notion of the world as a kind of collage. And I think that that is evident in the method of work – or the method of study – which is being used in this conference. Namely a series of discrete presentations put together in a kind of collage form where each lecture, or slide-show, or film, or discussion does not have any necessary relationship to anything that comes before it, or comes after it. It can be – and often needs to be – replaced at the last minute because somebody doesn't turn up, because someone has a change of plans, or people like John and me change our minds. But we are working in a collage – on the system of intellectual collage. And this is very clearly seen by the fact that photographic material, still photographs and films, are an essential part of the teaching and discussion situation here, that it seems natural that what people say be illustrated – and that itself is a complicated concept – by visual material, because this also lies in the nature of the photograph and tells us something about the way we are now approaching a learning situation, and the way we relate one part of our learning to another.

Also, as a series of discrete fragmented interchangeable parts subject to very different kinds of interpretations, there's a great deal to say – I'm focusing now on the notion of system, on the notion of collage, on the notion of fragment – there is of course a great deal to be said about the larger theme which is the relation of self and system. I would suggest to you that this has a certain quality of mirage about it – depending on our familiarity with a system. And I want, you know, from here on to be using these terms always in quotes – depending on our familiarity with a system. What we are choosing, what has been decided that we shall call a 'self' appears either in the foreground or the background. There is some I think implicit foreground, background, metaphor here as well which is illustrated in the green brochure where there are a number of visual illustrations of that concept.

In systems which are exotic to us, we have difficulty finding the self. I was in China last year and, as interesting as being in China and trying to understand what they were about, was being in the company of other foreigners – watching their efforts to find out what China was about, and the way they tried to understand things I'm talking about. Western Europeans and Americans, and the theme of their difficulties, and of their very questions about contemporary Chinese society was always 'Well, I see the system but where is the self?' And very often – depending on particular degrees of political information or political approach – they would conclude 'Well there's so much system, there isn't any self'! And then other people would say 'Yes, there's the self, you see, there it is, you know, it's in the foreground – the system is in the background but you can see the self emerging out of the system'. But what most people feel when they go to China where you have an exotic system – a system where the rules are not familiar to us – and they are rules very opposed to those of our own society. Then people have difficulty seeing the self at all.

I not only want to point this out to you. I want to argue. Perhaps this can be something that when John and I begin to talk together it will become clearer. I want ultimately to argue that this is a false problem, and this is a false dichotomy – that the questions that are raised by this pairing of concepts aren't finally very serious questions, and that they in fact mislead more than they inform. But nevertheless they are, the questions that are implicit in a great deal of intellectual discourse and of practical activity in our society right now. The whole series of therapeutic movements that have grown up in this society in the last ten years, the post Freudian kinds of therapy – the activities associated with Esalen are simply one very well-known example – are essentially dealing with this question. And I again want to suggest without yet having made my case that it's a false question; that is, here's this system in which the self according to this analysis is being inhibited – or crushed, or is ignorant of itself, or is not allowed, or afraid to use proper means of expression – therefore we have to strengthen the self to fight the system. We have to teach people how to be selves, and how to acknowledge their own selves. This is a very powerful intellectual current in this country and it is based on that pair – very strongly based on that pair of terms.

I'd like now to turn to, perhaps, some of the activities that have been going on here – in particular the use of visual materials in relation to oral, or written information. And what John and I wanted to begin in our discussion together in front of you – because we were talking about this yesterday, and last night, and this morning – was the use of photographs to make certain kinds of points so the relationship between photographs and text, photographs and political information, photographs and a certain moral point of view – with particular reference to the last event last night, which was the photographs of Don McCullin that most of you saw. I hope that most of you did see, after which John was supposed to show his BBC films and he didn't . . .

JOHN BERGER

(entering on stage)

> I think that if we try now to talk a bit about what happened last night – we're already making a step in a contrary direction to tendency, perhaps, of the events yesterday. That is to say that we are already being reflective about something that has happened, and about something which we share – we all experienced. So it's not a question of simply making a critique for the sake of being critical – certainly not a question of personalities. It's a question of examining the kind of experience that we had last night. And although, maybe, the circumstances here last night were somewhat unique, that experience is an experience that we are subjected to all the time. The kind of images that you were seeing last night occur continually in the press, on television, in the media . . .
>
> Now I would like to say one thing. When you think of the self in polarity to the system – like Susan was saying – the self is posed as an isolated unit by that polarity. Now something very similar actually happens in many of the photographs of McCullin that you saw last night. Without question, images – of war, exploitation, power – can and have played a positive role in increasing awareness. But only within certain limits. Most of those photographs last night actually showed moments of agony – an individual's agony, many thousands of miles away.
>
> Now what is important about an incident of agony is that it breaks the continuity of the person suffering it – the continuity of their life's time. That moment is isolated. That is one of the features of agony. And

they are isolated alone within it. If you happen to be there maybe there is something you can do – but whatever you do, it is only, as it were, to put up a hand over that wall which is that isolated terrible moment.

Now if you have a photograph of such a moment – and of course all photographs isolate the moment, but the choice of that moment which is in itself already isolated – you have a kind of double isolation. And what happens is that moment is then removed from process. It is an isolated moment like the isolated self in relation to the system. Because it is separate from process, it is very difficult to come to terms for another person – to come to terms with it. Actually, the only thing you can do to come to terms with it is through action if you happen to be there. To some degree you rush forward you do whatever is necessary – that is a way of coming to terms with it. But when we are passively sitting, looking at those images, there is absolutely damn all that we can do. And that is built in to that moment. We feel that. What does that feeling give us? Finally, it gives us a sense of impotence. Therefore, the effect of such images repeated – perhaps one, in isolation, is different, but when they are repeated, is actually to make us feel powerless before those events.

SUSAN SONTAG

I think there are two other things that might be said to illustrate this point. One is: try to imagine that commentary either not there at all – the voice of the photographer, Don McCullin. Let's say seeing those images with simply some information – perhaps another nature of captions, or intertitles, but no voice, not the voice of the photographer superimposed simultaneously, received with the images – and already your experience of the images would have been different. Because as we saw it last night, we saw a set of images that was part of the psychological – the personal biography of one man, a photographer. We heard all the time as we were watching his voice saying 'then I went here, then I saw that, then I felt this, then I wanted to do that, then I was horrified, by then I was inured and not so moved, then someone said this to me, then I went back to England, but then I wanted to go again to see more imperialist wars in Asia' – didn't he use that phrase? – 'and then I went somewhere else', and so on. The fact that his commentary was superimposed on the images made him the center of the experience – in other words we were seeing the images filtered through a Self, the quest of the photographer. And we were asked to look at those images not simply as a record of certain observations, but we were asked to look at them as a means of self-expression. This man is hooked on taking photographs, even takes them when he's seriously wounded and in great pain, and that personal obsession – that and those personal experiences – bracket and reduce all those images. If as I say that commentary had not been there – even with the same limitations of photographic seeing that John has been talking about – we still could have possibly paid more attention to the photographs, what the photographs were about, than we were able to do with his commentary present. Or even if the commentary had been there but let's say he had talked – he'd been here, Don McCullin – and talked first and then showed the images, or we had heard a tape – the soundtrack of the film – but played first not over the images, we would have had a very different experience.

Secondly, by the nature of the way in which those images were organised – which is both in terms of a certain chronology of events, and in terms of the autobiography of one person – the historical meaning of those photographs is already severely limited by the context and the repetitive theme of agony. The historical meaning of those photographs was completely wiped out. All struggles became identical. If you saw the series of photographs in which the photographer is in a Turkish village encircled by Greeks, and you have any interest in the struggle in Cyprus – as far as what we saw last night, there was no information about that struggle and one felt that the photographer could just as well have been in a Greek village surrounded by Turks. What he had to say, what he had to observe, what interested him to photograph had nothing to do with any concrete political evaluation – with any kind of historical information whatsoever. It had to do with a certain kind of aesthetic looking at the world. You see, he shows a photograph of a Black American soldier throwing what I assume is a hand grenade, and he also tells you – he gives you some information – that that soldier was, right after the photograph was taken, very severely wounded. He says 'here's a photograph of a beautiful Black soldier throwing a hand grenade'. When I saw this photograph, I realised it looked like, I don't know, a discus thrower in the Olympics. This is a way, a set of motivations for taking photographs, a way of evaluating them, and a way of presenting them, which completely wipes out any political or moral evaluation of the material that he's presenting.

JOHN BERGER

Just as those photographs, in the way they were presented, were robbed, or without a historical context, something happens in the reaction. Because what you then have is pain. Pain presented in Cyprus. Pain presented in Vietnam. Because it has no historical context, it becomes generalised. It actually – like everything that isn't placed in history – becomes part of nature. The distinction being that nature is more or less always there as a constant, it is part of the human condition. History is the creation of men. Men are responsible for history, they are not responsible for nature. And so this pain – and remember, that it is always pain inflicted by other men – becomes part of nature. Not to say exactly that it becomes natural, but it becomes part of nature. It becomes a constant of a human condition. And so what is the reaction to that? Reaction almost regardless of your personal stance towards this, because this is actually induced by the use of those images. Your reaction is to say 'that is happening – it isn't happening to me, the most that I can do is to make a charitable gesture towards it'. And so, far from assuming responsibility for that, this is something which happens to another to which you may, or may not, make a charitable gesture. Even that charitable gesture may be not, of course, in terms of money, may even be in terms of action. But it is still essentially the reaction of the person who says 'the poor are always with us'. It is an action which comes out of the segment which is morally defined by Christian charity – which is timeless, a-historical, and unpolitical.

SUSAN SONTAG

I didn't see all of the previous presentation here last night, but from what I understood it had a similar form. And I have seen the photographs that are on display – that is a series of photographs were shown of poverty in Latin America. And along with that an analysis was made and, not surprisingly, the end of that analysis – the very last words – the speaker quoted, as I remember, a coffee grower in San Salvador saying 'I don't see how this is going to change, I think the situation is hopeless, I think poverty is going to increase, I think the lot of these people cannot be improved'. And what the speaker said just before that was 'After giving all this information, I'm not going to come on – like Jacob Riis – with some simple solutions'. Jacob Riis as many of you know being probably the first person to do in any great depth, and with considerable talent as a photographer, a kind of combination of text and photographic images – and in his case of the poor in New York in the 1880s and 1890s – as a call to conscience and to change, and ameliorate the situation of the poor. And the speaker said, 'Listen, I'm not going to come on with simple solutions of how we can better the life of the poor, as Jacob Riss did. We have learned, you know, almost a century later that these problems are extremely complicated in fact they're probably insoluble.' And then he ended, as you remember, with the quotation from someone who lives in that area – presumably not someone, from the nature of the language of that quotation, who shares the lot of those people, because the quotation was in an educated language therefore he is presumably a middle class or upper-class person. But he said it's probably hopeless – if something can be done it will be extremely difficult and take a very long time, and probably nothing in fact can be done. So you watch those images, and there were even a couple of hisses in the audience – but very few. You watch those images. You saw that misery, that atrocity. It wasn't people in death agony, but it was another stage in that gallery of suffering in the world, from which we are exempted, in which we – as members of that very privileged minority – do not participate. We saw it. We looked at it. And we came away with a sense that it was probably hopeless – just as Don McCullin said at the end of, you know, the text that we heard with the images.

I hope to live long enough to see a time in which people learn to solve problems by other ways than killing each other, but I doubt very much if I will. He was assimilating all the struggles which he saw to a general phenomenon of human cruelty. Therefore, for instance, in the Biafra material we saw photographs of people – mostly children – dying. We did not have even really the information that this was a war. I mean that was understood and mentioned in the text, but we had static images of the victims, of the sufferers. And therefore what Biafra is about, what the struggle in Cyprus is about, what the various events in Vietnam are about, all become assimilated to something which is a quasi-natural event – man's cruelty to man. And although one may say one hopes to live to see a time in which people will not kill each other, will not inflict this kind of suffering, the photographer knows, and the majority of people in this audience know, or feel, that that's a pious dream and that this is not going to happen. People are going to go on being cruel to each other – and that becomes therefore part of human nature.

JOHN BERGER

I would like to add to that, this: I don't think that we're for one moment arguing for easy ready-made optimistic solutions. Because they don't exist and it is partly the rhetoric of those solutions which dominated so much political thinking and talking in the West up to '68, or even afterwards. It is perhaps the unmasking of that rhetoric which now allows a kind of stoical cynicism to have a certain credency. So we're not arguing for easy prefabricated solutions. Probably what has to happen first, oddly enough, is that one is truthful. There is a great illusion that information, in itself, is the truth. Actually the truth is the relation between a person and the world of which that information may be an aspect. So truth begins in that relationship, it doesn't begin simply in information as such – or in a photographic image as such. What the system, the media, continually do is to deny space. Space for thought, actually. Space for discovering what one's relationship to what is happening really is. Because it's a sequence like that . . .

(clapping hands)
> . . . until suddenly the noise stops.

(stopping then)

SUSAN SONTAG

(spontaneously)
> Like a set of photographs being flashed on one after another . . .

JOHN BERGER
> Yes . . .

(after a silence)
> . . . Even if one of those images which we saw last night had been shown, but I don't mind which one – and despite what I've said about that moment of agony and the limitations of taking photographs of such a thing – if one of those had been on that screen and had actually been held there for ten minutes, or perhaps longer, so that each of you faced with that began – not only looking at that – but questioning your relationship to it, this would actually be the beginning of searching for a political solution. Because this would be the beginning of seeing the political choices open to each one of you. And when I say this, I'm not suggesting that there were not many of you making that effort. What I am suggesting is that the procedure really preempted the possibility of that effort continuing.

SUSAN SONTAG
> So in a sense each photograph, in this kind of display – and again, I want to repeat what both John and I have said: we are using the McCullin film

because we saw it together last night, because we assume most of you saw it. There are thousands of examples like it and we are bombarded with this kind of information all the time, and this is the style of display all the time in galleries, on television, in magazines, in newspapers and so on. So this is just a convenient example which we've shared; it's not that this example is more that than many others that we might have chosen – what happens is that because of the nature of the format – the fact that there is no space, no time, that's predetermined, and that one thing follows another, that each thing is therefore replaced by the other – each thing is annihilated by what follows it and all things in a sense become the same. Whether it's images of agony, images of pain, images of poverty – whether it's images of beauty. Any kind of photographic display gives us (I think) the illusion of information, the illusion of compassion, the illusion of understanding. I think myself that the explanatory value of a photograph is in fact very, very low, that there is a photographic way of seeing and the way we see something in a photograph is very different from the way we see it face to face without the intervention of the camera. We've learned to look at photographs – photographs are relatively recent objects in the world, but there are probably more photographs than there are any other kind of object on the whole planet. You think of the amount of photographs that exist in the world today. Everyone takes them, everyone has them, everybody collects them, everybody looks at them. And there is this double world, this duplicate world, which has been created in the last hundred years – a kind of miniaturised world, a world that you can appropriate, acquire, put it in galleries. You put it in books, you put it in albums, and we relate to what is represented in those photographs very differently than we relate to the real events. To see a photograph of someone dead is very different from seeing someone dead. To see a film of an operation is very different from seeing an operation. And I don't mean necessarily to suggest that seeing necessarily distances you, in that seeing a photographed image is necessarily a less powerful experience. In some cases it's a more powerful experience, in fact. I have had exactly that situation a number of times in my own life. I have seen, witnessed an operation with acupuncture anesthesia in China, where I was next to the surgeon in white surgical gown myself and standing next to the table, and I saw the whole operation. I didn't feel particularly squeamish. I was able to watch. It was a major operation. I saw some months later the same operation in a film, and I found it very difficult to watch. I turned my eyes away several times and I felt slightly nauseated. That's a not an uncommon experience. You know, it doesn't necessarily mean – to repeat the point – that what you see in a photograph or in a film, you relate less strongly to than you would in real life. Sometimes you relate more strongly to it. But why? Because looking at a photographed image is different from looking at the real thing. It is a very special kind of looking and insofar, as we tie in our notion of information with that kind of information you get from the photographed world as opposed to the world, we are I think – indeed as John has suggested – increasing our impotence.

I want to make a further point, that John in what he just said used another form of the polarity. I had said 'self and system' is perhaps another version of the old polarity 'individual and society', and John used the terms 'person' and 'world'. Okay let's take those three sets of terms; there's a different feeling for each one of them. And I think 'person and world' is of all three by far the one that's most preferable. Because it closes the gap, a little bit. You see, 'self and system' sounds like 'are you going to be a cog in the machine, or aren't you'? That seems to be the kind of question that it's raising. 'Individual and society' also I think increases one's sense of impotence – well, we want to be individuals, we prize very much our sense of individuality and yet we know we're made by society, and ultimately we're shaped by society. So the question is only finding that margin of freedom that we can have, within the general imperatives of society – again, I think, a false way of putting the problem. The 'person and world', although not entirely satisfactory, I think is a bit more promising. Because a person is not outside the world. Every person is in a world, in a series of worlds. And it doesn't automatically lead us to the kind of reasoning which confirms both a pseudo-sophistication, a false idea of information – and ultimately a kind of humanistic or civilised resignation. I also want to repeat, in another way, John's point about information in itself not being valuable. What matters is the context. And what matters is the connection with ideas of action and if the notion of action, of praxis, is not examined if we don't examine the way we get information – what we do with information, and the whole acquisitive idea of information. So that information is itself simply another commodity like cars, or refrigerators, or television sets, or boats, or airplanes. We in fact are not learning to do anything with our information at all. We are simply learning to be a certain kind of person which fits in very well within an advanced capitalist society – a person who is intellectually mobile, tolerant, sophisticated, not too deeply rooted in any particular social situation that, you know, can be moved around by the corporation or the institution, can live abroad and not be completely at a loss in those situations of cultural transplant. We have an older idea of education or information in this country which had to do with acculturation, with taking people from many different cultures, and teaching them to be Americans. Now we're not so interested in the notion of acculturation because the society, and the means of production, and the whole international situation has changed. We're very interested in this country in making people more sophisticated. And the level of information in educational institutions and in the mass media is much higher, in quotes, than it was ten, or twenty, or thirty years ago. I think it's because a different kind of person is wanted now by this society. Someone as I say who is mobile, who is uprootable, whose roots are shallow, who is tolerant, who could roll with the punches, who can change, who can adapt, who can incorporate, who can dismantle one part of the system and replace it with another part – so the kind of modernist undertakings that have now become standard – in conferences of this kind, at better universities, in the mass media – are not, I think – though we often imagine them to be – critical of the society, of the ruling ideas of the society. They, in fact, reinforce them.

(applause)

JOHN BERGER

Exactly. We do not want to take up all the time allotted us, to allow a certain space for you to consider your reactions to what we've been saying. This afternoon we can continue along the same kind of theme, hopefully with more of a dialogue – because with probably fewer people.

(both leaving stage to applause)

MODERATOR

(on microphone, introducing CORNELL CAPA)

Don't move. One of the exciting things that happens when you're lucky at a conference like that, is that the collage takes . . .

[Afternoon recording not found]

The *Free* Aspen Flyer

Saturday, June 22, 1974

IWA

PHOTOGRAPHIC WRAP-UP

...er Bobby Seale had defined the
...m" as "the universe" and
...pping out of the system" as a clear
...ibility, the IDCA settled down to
...re the question "what is the role of
...graphy?"
...san Sontag, John Berger, and
...ell Capa had the debate, and as
... nothing was resolved.
... Flyer photo staff supplies two
...ers of their own. One—the pur-
... of photography is to fill the white
... left over when all the ads are
printed.
And two—the purpose of
photography is to keep photographers
from starving like the subjects of their
photographs.
(Honest, folks, we're not cynical,
just hungry. And three issues a week
doesn't leave much time for debate.)
EDITOR'S NOTE: All photos in this
issue (with the exception of the cover)
are by award-winning Aspen photo-
journalist Doug Lee. Cover photo by
Chris Cassatt.

Susan Sontag

Cornell Capa

John Berger

Milton Glaser

Epilogue

Benoît Bourreau

Sadly, there are no other recordings from Aspen, no more than there are any of the emails likely exchanged after the turn of the century. There are, however, works that respond to each other, sometimes across intervals of several years. For instance, those about AIDS, with Susan Sontag's short story 'The Way We Live Now' in 1986 and John Berger's novel *To the Wedding* in 1995. There are also parallel, concomitant political engagements in support of local struggles, such as Chiapas for John Berger and Sarajevo for Susan Sontag. It was following in those footsteps that John Berger visited Palestine for the first time in 2003, while in 2001, Susan Sontag had just received the Jerusalem Prize for the Freedom of the Individual in Society.

Faced with the world's pain, such connections reveal the similar empathy of these two writers. Despite time and distance, there is also a shared attentiveness, a certain tact and care, a familial support almost, summed up in October 2022 by Yves Berger in a filial email to David Rieff: 'I have this image of each of them being for one another a sparkle that lit vast domains of unexplored thinking for their wild minds.'

In this spirit, Susan Sontag sought several times to invite John Berger to the University of Cornell, where she taught, and recommended his eldest son, Jacob, to art critic Annette Michelson for a seminar at the Tisch School of the Arts in New York. Their generosity also took other guises, gifts countering absence with the sending of wine or a book of poetry, a rapport that intrigues David Rieff to this day: 'I often wondered, contemplating their friendship – I knew John glancingly, and only observed him and my mother in each other's company two or three times, so what I am saying may be the proverbial nonsense on stilts – that I was surprised they were not closer still. But perhaps they were too alike, yet not alike enough.'

Susan Sontag and John Berger's fateful first meeting in Aspen occurred during Berger's one and only trip to the United States; on that occasion he and his wife Beverly also visited her family in Virginia before settling down in Mieussy in the French Alps. It was there that Susan Sontag would visit them several times in the late 1970s, alternating these visits with meetings in London in the early 1980s, then again once or twice in the early 1990s. There was intimacy in their artistic and literary complicity which went well beyond intellectual seduction, which John Berger summed up in his letter from 1 August 1990 by referring to Susan Sontag's 1987 autobiographical short story, 'Pilgrimage, Tea with Thomas Mann' where she writes of her formative years with her sidekick Merrill in 1947: 'We are very different but we come from the same place – and what you write now takes me back there'. Evoking a common imaginary past, John Berger's words are proof of a feeling of shared destiny, as well as an unwavering reciprocal admiration; a sentiment further confirmed many years earlier by Susan Sontag in the postscript to a letter dated 21 March 1975 in which she alludes to a rereading of *G*.

Geographical proximity likely led to more regular meetings in France as Susan Sontag began to spend long periods at the home of the film producer Nicole Stéphane in Paris to carry out research on Walter Benjamin's *Das Passagen-Werk* (*The Arcades Project*). Likewise, Benjamin's work *Der Erzähler* (*The Storyteller*) can be seen as one of the references informing the title of their discussion for *Voices*. And in equal measure to Benjamin, that *flâneur* of Parisian arcades, one must not forget the influence of Roland Barthes, whose *La Chambre Claire* (*Camera Lucida*) was published in 1980. Even more fundamental perhaps is Bertolt Brecht, whom John Berger quotes that same year in his essay 'Uses of Photography – For Susan Sontag', substituting the word *acting* with the word *photography* in lines taken from 'Darstellung von Vergangenheit und Gegenwart in einem' ('Portrayal of Past and Present in One'), in *Poems 1913–1956*:

So you should simply make the Instant
Stand out, without in the process hiding
What you are making it stand out from. Give your acting
That progression of one-thing-after-another, that attitude of
Working up you what you have taken on. In this way
You will show the flow of events and also the course
Of your work, permitting the spectator
To experience this Now on many levels, coming from Previously and
Merging into Afterwards, also having much else now
Alongside It. He is sitting not only
In your theatre but also
In the world.

Filmed in real time, with no retakes except during the three technical cuts, is this not what Susan Sontag and John Berger achieve in *To Tell a Story*? What appears as the acme of an intense relationship unfolds live, on camera. With the poise of an actor, he introduces her – only for her to contradict him. And so their conversation volleys back and forth, carrying us, the audience, along in their playfully rebounding dialectics, ceaselessly holding us captive.

There is also this playful quality in the inaugural conference by Susan Sontag and John Berger at IDCA. But beyond its tone and content, this first public appearance in Aspen founded their respective viewpoints in the same reading of the world and its representations. A faith in modernity that they will both amend but never in quite the same fashion as each other. It would take John Berger long months and several attempts, with the help of the faithful Anthony Barnett, before publishing a first review of *On Photography* in 1978 in the New York magazine *Seven Days*, entitled, 'Photography: God of The Instant', from which is taken the frequently cited: 'Susan Sontag has written a book of great importance and originality . . . All future discussion or analysis on the role of photography in the affluent mass-media societies are now bound to begin with her book.'

There remains no trace, however, of the origin of Susan Sontag's famous words: a simple endorsement likely written upon request for the publisher Tom Engelhardt at Pantheon, that she copied in a response letter dated 24 February 1980 to John Berger. It is impossible to mistake the sincerity, even granting the usual exaggeration of the exercise: 'I admire and love John Berger's books. He writes about what is important, not just interesting – in contemporary English letters, he seems to be peerless; not since Lawrence has there been a writer who offers such attentiveness to the sensual world with responsiveness to the imperatives of conscience. He is a wonderful artist and thinker.'

Thirty years after their first meeting, John Berger learned of Susan Sontag's death from leukaemia on 28 December 2004. She whom he had almost always known adorned with a silver streak in her hair, emblem of chemotherapy that she had worn as a badge of victory since 1975, pushed back the cancer yet again in 1998. It was doubtless from this distinctive characteristic that he attributed to her the affectionate nickname that he recalled in an email to the actress Tilda Swinton in September 2010, suggesting a game of ping pong for a scene in the shooting of the film *The Seasons in Quincy – Four Portraits of John Berger*: 'It's what Silver (Susan Sontag) and I liked doing best.'

Their passion for table tennis illuminates an almost jubilatory aspect to the relationship between Susan Sontag and John Berger. It is no doubt also a metaphor for the surprise and joy of a deep mutual recognition, a feeling recalled in the tribute he addressed in an email to their mutual friend Maria Nadotti on the morning of 30 December 2004:

Quicksilver

Susan Sontag – quicksilver darting between past and future to shed light on the otherwise dark present – and your conscience that travelled almost at the speed of light.

I recall playing ping-pong with you and your fast services, and your laughter, which was always about surprise.
One surprise prompting another. Twenty all. Your service.
And the flick of your wrist, which looked so young, and which long, long before had already been an example for your mind that later grasped the world.

Quicksilver, liquid metal, nickname for Mercury, keeper of eloquence and dexterity, protector of roads, deliverer of the messages we need.

Game and set to you, Quicksilver.

Acknowledgements

I would like to extend my warmest thanks to David Rieff, Katya Berger Andreadakis, Jacob Berger and Yves Berger for their unwavering trust and support throughout my journey. My heartfelt thanks also go to Simon McBurney, Tilda Swinton, Gareth Evans, Maria Nadotti and Paul Edwards for their initial comments and feedback. I would also like to express my gratitude to Tom Overton, Béatrice Mousli, Benjamin Moser, Anthony Barnett, Michael Dibb and Christopher Sheppard for shedding light on my research. This collection would not have been possible without the crucial assistance of Teresa Pintó at Carmen Balcells and Tracy Bohan at the Wylie Agency. Finally, I would like to acknowledge the invaluable help of Lily Robert-Foley, Claire Reiderman and Vicki Rutherford in editing this project. Readers now have a story to tell.

Benoît Bourreau,
January 2026

Image Credits

Voices Opening Credits; John Berger (Close Up); Susan Sontag (Close Up). Stills from 'To Tell a Story', *Voices* (1983) © Brook Lapping Productions/Channel 4. Courtesy of the BFI National Archive.

John Berger and Susan Sontag's letters (1975–98). Facsimiles of correspondence © John Berger Estate and Susan Sontag Estate. Courtesy of the John Berger and Susan Sontag Estates.

IDCA Programme Book Cover (1974); IDCA Statement for 'Between Self & System'; IDCA Speakers Portraits (The Free Aspen Flyer). International Design Conference in Aspen records, Getty Research Collections. © J. Paul Getty Trust. Courtesy of J. Paul Getty Trust.